# GUIDANCE MONOGRAPH SERIES

SHELLEY C. STONE

BRUCE SHERTZER

*Editors*

## GUIDANCE MONOGRAPH SERIES

The general purpose of Houghton Mifflin's Guidance Monograph Series is to provide high quality coverage of topics which are of abiding importance in contemporary counseling and guidance practice. In a rapidly expanding field of endeavor, change and innovation are inevitably present. A trend accompanying such growth is greater and greater specialization. Specialization results in an increased demand for materials which reflect current modifications in guidance practice while simultaneously treating the field in greater depth and detail than commonly found in textbooks and brief journal articles.

The list of eminent contributors to this series assures the reader expert treatment of the areas covered. The monographs are designed for consumers with varying familiarity to the counseling and guidance field. The editors believe that the series will be useful to experienced practitioners as well as beginning students. While these groups may use the monographs with somewhat different goals in mind, both will benefit from the treatment given to content areas.

The content areas treated have been selected because of specific criteria. Among them are timeliness, practicality, and persistency of the issues involved. Above all, the editors have attempted to select topics which are of major substantive concern to counseling and guidance personnel.

*Shelley C. Stone*
*Bruce Shertzer*

# ESTABLISHING GUIDANCE PROGRAMS IN SECONDARY SCHOOLS

**ANTHONY C. RICCIO**
OHIO STATE UNIVERSITY

**JOSEPH J. QUARANTA**
UNIVERSITY OF TOLEDO

**HOUGHTON MIFFLIN COMPANY · BOSTON**
NEW YORK · ATLANTA · GENEVA, ILL. · DALLAS · PALO ALTO

# CONTENTS

# EDITORS' INTRODUCTION

In this monograph Professors Riccio and Quaranta forthrightly set forth the factors which must be considered in establishing guidance programs within secondary schools. Beginning with a discussion of the purposes of guidance in education, an overview of the secondary school as a social system, and an examination of the students for whom the educational enterprise exists, the authors proceed to material bearing on the counselor as an individual and the establishment and implementation of program objectives. The final chapter of the monograph treats the problem of program evaluation and emphasizes the necessity of building such efforts into the initial stages of programs.

Detailed consideration of all of the above factors is mandatory for those who intend to establish functional and meaningful guidance services. As the authors clearly demonstrate, the task is not simple nor is it a one step procedure in the sense that it is once performed and then dismissed as accomplished.

The material presented in this monograph is intended to serve as a basic guide to those involved in the crucial steps of initiating new programs. The discerning reader will find within it more than a sequence of steps. He will find a rationale to serve as a base for his professional actions. Because such a rationale is imbedded in the material, it can also serve productively as a means for assessing existing programs.

SHELLEY C. STONE

BRUCE SHERTZER

# The Role of Guidance in the Educational Setting

Effecting behavioral change is the purpose of all educational endeavors. Each educational agency and its component services attempts to assist the individual student to become a better individual primarily as a result of exposure to and participation in a series of structured experiences. Educational experiences are intended to help an individual student move from less desirable toward more desirable performance on a given behavioral dimension. The function of education is to identify the developmental level of an individual student on a number of behavioral dimensions and to institute programs to improve his development in these areas.

Essentially, the school program is concerned with helping to effect three kinds of behavioral change: cognitive change, affective change, and conative change. Each of these changes is described briefly below.

1. *Cognitive Change.* The first kind of change that the school attempts to effect relates to knowledge and intellectual development. Obviously, if a school program is successful, the individual student will be more knowledgeable each year as he participates in the program. The vast majority of students completing a school program should possess sufficient relevant knowledge to play an effective role in American society. A democratic society, more than any other, is dependent upon an informed and knowledgeable citizenry.

The school has been selected by society as the primary agent to develop an informed citizenry. The school must help the student to learn how to evaluate his environment, to make sense out of the plethora of information directed at him through the various mass media of communication. The school assists the individual to appreciate the American heritage and helps him to acquire a frame of reference within which he can assess and accept or reject current phenomena.

2. *Affective Change.* Knowledge is powerful, but it is not useful to society unless it is directed toward noble ends. A knowledgeable demagogue is a far greater threat to our way of life than is an illiterate thug. The school, therefore, must also concern itself with helping students to acquire a set of ideals which will encourage them to put their knowledge to good use. The school, therefore, is interested in helping students to acquire a set of ideals that are in keeping with American tradition, so that they will act on the basis of ideals rather than on the basis of selfishness or impulse.

3. *Conative Change.* Knowledge and ideals are necessary but not sufficient characteristics of an effective citizen. The effective citizen also makes a positive contribution to the economy of the nation. With the help of the school and perhaps other educational agencies, he acquires saleable skills. The utilization of these skills in later life makes it possible for an individual to enjoy economic security and to support himself and his loved ones.

Briefly, then, the school has three basic objectives: (1) it attempts to help students become less ignorant and more knowledgeable; (2) it attempts to help students act less on the basis of self-interest and impulse and more on the basis of ideals; and (3) it attempts to help students become economically efficient by helping them to translate their native capacities into productive abilities. Since these changes are to take place within the same individual, there is obviously a considerable amount of overlap in the manner in which these changes are realized.

Granted the validity of the behavioral changes listed above, it follows that a school program or a school activity is desirable or valuable to the extent that it assists the school to realize its objectives. Specifically, a guidance program makes sense to the extent that it helps students acquire the changes listed above. But it must be remembered that although guidance services are relevant to cognitive, affective, and conative change, these services are most relevant to the production of affective change. Affective changes are concerned with helping a student to understand himself in terms of his assets and his liabilities, his aspirations and his concerns. Further, the student is to be helped to see the relevance of these factors to the world in which he must function.

In this monograph, therefore, guidance is defined as a process, developmental in nature, by which an individual is assisted to understand, accept, and utilize his abilities, aptitudes, interests, and attitudinal patterns in relation to his aspirations. The authors believe, purely and simply, that the major purpose of guidance services is to assist students to make appropriate decisions. Emphasis in this definition is placed upon the conception of guidance as a process, the process of acquiring as much knowledge as possible about factors relevant to the making of a decision and then *utilizing* this knowledge in making decisions. Guidance services are a structured attempt to assist young people to develop the habit of making appropriate decisions.

### Assumptions Undergirding Guidance Services

The concept of guidance services is predicated upon two major assumptions: (1) man has dignity and worth and is therefore worthy of study and assistance; (2) man is not completely self-sufficient and needs assistance in resolving a number of critical problems which confront him throughout his life-span. These metaphysical assumptions are the *reason why* guidance services make sense.

The concept of the dignity and worth of man is derived from several different philosophical stances. Some would say that the dignity of man is a first principle and therefore not susceptible to question or explanation. Pragmatically speaking, the concept is essential to the continued existence of a democratic society. Others hold, in conformity with the Judaic-Christian tradition, that man has dignity and worth because he is made in the image and likeness of a personal God. It would appear essential to the very nature of their work that all counselors accept the dignity and worth of the individual. The philosophical commitments of the counselor which lead him to accept this dictum are another matter. In a pluralistic society, men will never arrive at a consensus on basic metaphysical questions, nor does such agreement seem necessary. One's stand on *ultimate* questions does not prevent him from working effectively with colleagues who subscribe to different positions on such matters — provided both can agree on such *operational* concepts as the dignity and worth of all students. To expect a school counselor to subscribe to given positions on ultimate questions is in effect to establish a religious test for entry into the profession.

Complex societal forces make it impossible for most individuals to resolve the difficulties confronting them throughout life without receiving some assistance from other individuals. The incredibly rapid rate at which changes are taking place in society and the impact of these changes as they influence the choices confronting individuals is of great moment to school counselors. Below are brief statements relating the impact of these changes on the role expectancies of school personnel.

1. *Home Life.* With both parents away from home more than ever before, the home no longer has the training function it once had in the lives of boys and girls. Functions which were performed by parents are more frequently fulfilled by parent-surrogates. Teachers and counselors are often asked to fulfill what in the past were viewed as parental roles.

2. *The World of Work.* As a result of the fantastic technological developments occurring almost daily in the world, it has been stated that a significant portion of youth currently enrolled in school will spend their adult lives pursuing occupations which do not as yet exist. Students will need assistance in preparing themselves for the vocational choices they will be compelled to make in a changing world.

3. *Changes in Rates of Birth and Death.* The fluctuations in our birth rate influence the kind of services that society will need and the kinds of problems that will confront individuals. For example, as a result of the increased birth rates in the post-World War II period, it has become increasingly difficult for good students to gain admission to our more prestigious private universities. Similarly, the impact of modern medical practice on longevity creates problems for young adults who must assume responsibility for their older kin. Individuals need assistance from school, private, and community agencies in planning to meet the problems arising from our changing rates of birth and death.

4. *Increased Need for Education.* As our society becomes more technological in nature, there will be an increased demand for trained manpower. School dropouts will become a more severe problem than ever before. Society will require trained personnel to help youth make the most of their educational opportunities so that they can assume productive roles in our economy.

5. *Increased Leisure Time.* Technological innovations will make it possible for individuals to have more leisure time in the future. Youth will need assistance in acquiring avocations that will help them make worthwhile use of the increased amount of leisure they will be afforded.

6. *Changing Educational Philosophies.* Changing world conditions are reflected in school programs and in the decisions made by boards of education and state educational agencies. Students need assistance in making sense out of the educational programs established for them.

These are but six examples of the kinds of social changes that precipitate problems for youngsters which they may have difficulty in resolving without assistance. School personnel, especially school counselors, will undoubtedly assume more importance in the lives of students as these and other social changes impinge upon the lives of students with ever-increasing intensity.

But guidance does not just happen. It must be planned. The school which is committed to helping students learn how to make appropriate decisions must establish services to realize this objective. These services are as follows:

1. The school must have some means of determining how each student differs from other students in the school on pertinent variables such as abilities, aptitudes, interests, and attitudes. The focus in this service is *acquiring data about the individual* and is referred to as the appraisal service.

2. The school must have some means of informing the student about the demands and expectations of his school environment as well as of the larger society of which the school is but a part. The student must be informed of scholastic and occupational requirements and of the relationships existing among them. This service is called the information service.

3. The school must provide an opportunity for the student to discuss with trained personnel the relevance of the material comprising the appraisal service and the information service to the life-situation of the particular student. This service is the counseling service.

4. The school must help the student to set in motion the course of action he has decided to take. This service makes it possible for the student to be placed in a certain class or on a certain job, as well as to take advantage of a pertinent community resource. This service is called the placement service.

5. In addition to these services, the school must also provide some means for determining the effectiveness of the services it is providing. The student is seldom concerned directly with this research and evaluation service other than as a respondent to questionnaires and the like, but the research and evaluation engaged in by appropriate school personnel play a large role in renovating and modifying the guidance services with which students are directly concerned.

Much of the remainder of this monograph is concerned with how the services listed above are related to effecting behavioral change on the part of the students. But before a school counselor can seriously begin to consider how these services might be implemented, he must consider three very important variables related to the establishment and success of any guidance endeavor. First, he must be able to view the school as a social system, a system with characteristics which must be understood if he is to attempt to introduce any innovative programs which in any way alter the system. Second, he must be conversant with recent thought on the product with which he will be working — the student, the adolescent; and he must realize that although these adolescents have much in common, his business is to pay especially careful attention to the ways in which they differ from each other. Third, he must know and understand himself and his colleagues, especially in terms of why and how they have become counselors. The next three chapters of this monograph are devoted to a consideration of recent thought on these crucial variables. The last two chapters are devoted to a treatment of the principles and techniques involved in implementing and evaluating guidance services in the light of insights acquired about the school, the adolescent, and the counselor.

# 2

# The Secondary School

The institutional setting in which the counseling and guidance activities occur will determine to a large extent the nature of these activities. The institution prescribes the clientele, the purpose of the encounters, the climate, the supportive resources, and to some degree the ultimate outcomes. Counseling and guidance represent helping relationships incorporated in many institutional settings; the nature of these relationships is therefore in large part determined by the institution. In an effective institution the operations undertaken are all compatible one with the other and are all in keeping with the basic purpose of the institution itself. Mathewson (1967) sees the educational institutions as those which should be the primary agents of the guidance function in our society. He points out that education is the one universal institution able to think of the individual and of society in terms of their welfare rather than in terms of itself. He further explains that education provides the most favorable climate for helping individuals to assist themselves. Although objectives of education and the objectives of guidance are in most cases compatible, the school counselor cannot rest assured that establishing a guidance program will meet with automatic success.

The school counselor, in establishing his program, will need to recognize the dynamics of his own school and the behavioral systems as well as the needs of the personnel within it.

## The School as a Social System

As a singular example of interpersonal behavior within a social structure, the establishment of a guidance program in the secondary school can be viewed through the dynamics of social processes. As such, the school counselor is attempting to organize various elements of an existing system, the educational program, into a planned sub-system, the guidance program. He is attempting, moreover, to pro-mulgate change within an existing educational structure which gen-erally resists change. Thus, understanding the dynamics of social structures, the influencing process, and principles of re-education will contribute to the counselor's understanding of his task, the setting in which this task occurs, and his implementation of it.

### Social Processes

Social structures exist and can be examined as largely independent from the individuals who function within them. By utilizing a social framework for observing human behavior in the school, the counselor can attain an objectivity free of the distortions inherent in personal, subjective examinations of behavior. He can separate and examine what is from what ought to be. A large proportion of the behavior of the individuals within the school can be determined and, even more important, predicted on the basis of these concepts.

Social structures consist of a set of *positions*, the implementation of which constitutes a set of legitimate, mutually expected behaviors involving *rights* and *obligations* among individuals. This pattern fol-lows a more or less definite set of rules (Secord and Backman, 1964). Thus the teacher role carries a specific set of rights relative to the role of administrator or student and in turn must be fulfilled by dis-charging certain teacher obligations. Each position has a certain status within the school which differs from that of others. The school coun-selor, in establishing a guidance program, must recognize and accept his role as well as those of others. In a given school the symbols of status are an integral part of the system. Usually these include salary differential, flexible time schedule, private office facilities, secretarial help, proximity to administrative center, authority over others in spe-cific activities (such as testing), and additional training or certifica-tion. The implication of these symbols of status for the school coun-selor are obvious and should be clearly understood in terms of social processes.

In addition to rights, each position carries certain obligations rela-tive to each other position. The anticipation of this *role performance* or *role behavior* constitutes *role expectations*. These role expectations are in a large part determined by the perceptions and the needs of reciprocal roles or counter positions. Role expectation, then, defines how a person should behave, while role performance describes how he does behave. The counselor should understand the system of internal and external sanctions by which expected behavior is rewarded and unexpected behavior is punished. This reward system can be highly personal and subtle and can be defined in many ways.

Once set into operation, the system will generally function as established. When a new position is added to a system it causes others to wonder not only what *it* is but also who *they* are. The implications for change are dramatic. If the assumptions are made that change is inherently threatening and that individuals strive for consistency, the forces for changing counselor role or adding a guidance program to an existing educational structure are far outweighed by the forces for status quo.

The structural need of a social system to maintain itself provides at the same time the valuable characteristic of predictability and the frustrating trait of resistance to change. The capacity to develop a wide repertoire of role performances within legitimate expectations contributes to effective job performance as well as to general mental health. The ability to accurately perceive role expectations must be highly developed in one who proposes to bring about change in a social system. Both of these need to be developed by the school counselor establishing a guidance program within an existing school program.

Social systems are not free from conflict. Conflict can occur in at least three ways: *role-role conflict, self-role conflict,* and *role ambiguity* (Sarbin, 1954). In the first, two divergent sets of rights and obligations form the expectation of a role to be enacted by a single person. The teacher-counselor position can be an example of this type of conflict. Expectations of teacher differ significantly from expectations of counselor. This may include differences in what should be included in the role, the range of behavior allowed, the situation where it applies, whether mandatory or preferred, or the hierarchy of role behavior. Often the school counselor is expected to combine incompatible traits in the same role. He is expected to be sensitive, nurturant, and introspective as a counselor, as well as aggressive, organized, and authoritarian as program developer.

The self-role conflict occurs when an individual finds role obligations incompatible with his own characteristics and self concept. He is expected to be and is treated as a kind of person dissimilar from his own characteristics and different from the person he perceives himself to be. Yet this role is defined by the social organization and must be implemented as nearly as possible within those limits. Where counselor is defined in a school setting contrary to the way the individual assuming the position perceives himself, implementation of the role produces tension and frustration.

Role ambiguity occurs where rights and obligations are not clearly or consistently defined. Since one's own position is determined in relation to that of others and vice versa, such ambiguity deeply affects others as well. While at times useful, ambiguity of the school counselor's role in the social structure can be disruptive and must be evaluated in terms of desired social outcomes. Role conflict or role strain is not perceived by all behavioral scientists as necessarily unfortunate nor unusual. Goode (1960) sees role strain as a required circumstance in the dynamic of individual-institution interaction. The individual bargains for his own role behavior, and it is this bargaining system which gives social organization its strength. Goffman (1961) sees the resolution of role in terms of a compromise which is also a necessary part of the social system. Nevertheless, the resolution of role conflict requires considerable energy, much of which could be better applied to role enactment. The tensions, frustration, and even hostility accompanying role conflict can often go undiagnosed if social processes are ignored.

Studies of school counselor role have dealt primarily with role perceptions and role expectations as viewed from reciprocal roles of parent, teacher, and student. The evidence is accumulating that the current situation regarding the role of the school counselor in the secondary school is at best nebulous. Disparate perceptions between the role as anticipated through counselor education and the role in the actual school setting create a situation where role-role conflict, self-role conflict, and role ambiguity are inevitable. Efforts on the part of counselor educators and the profession itself to give direction in the confusion are heartening. Yet the behavior of related personnel and students in the work setting of the school counselor will continue to respond to rules of social organization.

### Power and Influence Structures

The overt power structure of the school is usually specified in a written description of line and staff relationships. This is usually accompanied by a statement of distribution of roles and responsibilities among the staff. Procedures for making decisions and channels for communication are spelled out, and a system of recruiting and orienting newcomers is usually included. This formal description of the organization constitutes the institutionalization of the social system. It includes a power structure but does not always explain all of the influencing relationships. A number of other formal organizations and informal systems can influence the school. Community organizations, the church, and related school groups can bring about change or determine action. Informal groups within the community or among the students also have an impact.

Within any group there are shared perceptions of those who are leaders and those who are followers. These individuals and groups form an influence structure as effective as the formal one. The school counselor needs to recognize the formal organization and its overt power structure and utilize it legitimately. He also must recognize the influence structures which have great impact upon the total school and particularly upon changes in the structure. The former are often dealt with in organization and administration courses included as a part of the school counselor's training. The latter constitute a more subversive, often illusive element and exist more or less illegitimately in the eyes of the educational theorists. Nonetheless, behavior vital to the establishment of a guidance program will defy explanation without utilizing these concepts of power and influence structures (Secord and Backman, 1964).

### Bureaucratization

The ASCA Proposed Statement of Policy for Secondary School Counselors and Guidelines for Implementation of Policy (1964) specifically recognizes the inherent dichotomy between the individual and the institution, the person and the social system. In defining the professional rationale relative to the school, the Proposed Statement of Policy contends that

> Because the school is a democratic institution using group objectives and methods, and because learning, maturing, and self-realization are inevitably individual processes, a paradox or conflict for the student is implicit within our education structure. Therefore, the school counselor recognizes such conflict as a natural part of the educative processes in a democracy and sees the mediation of this conflict as a very important part of his role.

This inherent paradox exists universally but becomes even more acute under certain circumstances. As the school increases in size and the hierarchy of formally defined positions becomes more rigidly established, and as increased specialization occurs, bureaucratization results. The system becomes less responsive to the individuals who comprise it. The behavior of teachers and other school personnel, as well as students, follows the dictates of the bureaucracy. School structure becomes formal, objective, logical, and efficient. Rules and regulations are expanded and enforced to improve predictability. Individuals in the system become specialized and lose perspective of the total operation. Authority is a complex and rigid hierarchy. The structure supersedes the person, and the needs of the institution demand conformity and depersonalization. Interchangeability of parts, that is teachers, students, administrators, and counselors, from one system to the next or from one year to the next, becomes an asset (Goslin, 1965).

Where such a process has progressed extensively, the establishment of a guidance program faces unique problems. The program is expected to fit into the existing structure with the least possible binding. Most of the outcomes of the program are institutional and are already defined. The efficacy of guidance is rated in terms of these prescribed goals. The counselor need not let his person emerge in order to be successful, and to the degree that he lets subjectivity enter his work he can be inefficient. While a counselor may choose not to implement his program in such a manner as to perpetuate the bureaucracy but acts so as to change it, it behooves him to clearly understand the rules of social organization that he is violating. He must accurately anticipate the consequences.

### Preachment Versus Practice

One of the most salient characteristics of the American society is the obvious discrepancy between preachment and practice. The society appears to hold values which are useless as guides for understanding human behavior. This is true both in regard to the general American culture and the most intimate of relationships within it. A part of this phenomenon can be attributed to the national trait of holding up ideals, many of which are often unattainable. Another part can be explained in terms of the discrepancy between individual aims and the institutionalization of the means to attain them. The latter is particularly true in the educational situation.

Washburne (1964) points out that educational theory can not only become separate from educational structure but conflict can occur. He suggests a number of potential conflict elements within the opposing directions taken by bureaucratic structure and modern educational theory.

1. *Individual Versus Mass.* Efficient bureaucracies want to treat all units the same, develop standard operating procedure and leave little room for unique responses. Theory describes each individual as unique, with unique problems and responses which demand specialized treatment.

2. *Necessary Time Versus Fixed Time.* The bureaucracy tends toward fixed time limits for a particular task with instruction divided into a time schedule more or less rigidly adhered to. Theory is concerned

with the ends and with individual learning rates. Flexibility of scheduling is desired to plan the educational experience around the learner not the institution.

3. *Creativity Versus Predictability.* The bureaucratic school values predictability. This is accomplished through rules and regulations, discipline, promptness, memory work and facts. It passively or actively discourages variances from the norm, creativity, unanticipated events and criticism. Creative ventures, on the other hand, flow from unstructured situations and divergent thinking. They are unpredictable.

4. *Unmeasurable Versus Measurable.* Creative behavior is often unmeasurable by current standards, yet such behavior should be allowed and rewarded. The bureaucracy concentrates on the measurable and values the objective test. Convergent thinking is required and such learning rewarded.

5. *Qualities Versus Quantities.* Educational theory based upon individualistic principles, responses and situations is concerned with qualities. Uniqueness of the individual can not be reduced to variations in degree on a few variables. Bureaucracy requires order and regulation and would tend to reduce the qualitative differences to quantitative ones.

6. *Unique Versus Formal.* The rules and regulations of a bureaucracy integrate individuals into classes or types and subtle and variable phenomena are ignored. The structure is imposed from above and those in direct contact with the individuals follow the dictates of those removed from the setting.

7. *Whole Versus Segmental.* Bureaucracies demand segmentalization and specialization. Students are dealt with in limited contact and the structure of content dictates the nature of the contact. Educational theory stresses the interrelationship of all knowledge and the dynamic characteristic of learning. Deeper involvement with the learner as a person is required for truly effective learning to occur. Bureaucracies prevent this. (Washburne, 1964)

The school counselor should recognize the extent to which his school is becoming bureaucratized. The dimensions stated above serve as one tool for examining the educational experiences as structured by the school. The discrepancy between preachment and practice should be noted, and the extent to which the staff engages in pretense should be observed. It should be clear that pretense is necessary for one to maintain a sense of professionalism and ego enhancement. It should not be attacked without provision for an adequate substitute.

Moreover, guidance often demands an allegiance to the concepts of educational theory which far surpasses that of the teacher. In counselor training, the individual takes precedence over the educational group. While much attention is paid to these same concepts in teacher training, in practice the school counselor role is flexibly structured so as to provide for individuality to a greater degree than is possible for the teacher. Thus the situation exists wherein individualization is considered a requisite by all staff members but is attainable only by some. Those who are unable to perform as they desire may resist others who can. The application of guidance concepts in an unreceptive setting can be difficult. The school counselor should be exceptionally keen in observing the discrepancy between word and deed and in determining the degree of bureaucratization of the school.

# 3

# The Student

The secondary school student is the major recipient of the guidance services in the secondary school. In numbers he comprises a group of thirteen and one-third million individuals, attends some thirty-one thousand secondary schools, and keeps some eight-hundred and fifty thousand professionals busily engaged in classroom teaching alone. Over twenty-seven and one-half billion dollars are spent each year on secondary school education, with another five billion added in capital outlay ("Magnitude," 1966). But the student cannot be described in numbers alone. He has an individuality which affords him his own unique characteristics, goals, problems, and potentials. He functions within his own social setting, which will determine more or less the realization of his potential. As a group he currently comprises one of the most influential subcultures in our society and is rapidly becoming even more influential.

The school counselor must be able to view the student from a number of different points of view. These different frameworks will in many ways determine what the counselor will do with the student, what sets of services will be brought to bear, and in what kinds of activities he will be engaged. The counselor must first view the student as an adolescent and see him from several vantages within the general framework. He must view him as a student both in the generic sense of the word and in terms of special considerations. At all times the counselor must be aware of the implications of his perceptual stance in the total development of the student.

## The Student as an Adolescent

The student in the secondary school is primarily an adolescent, secondarily a student. Adolescence has been variously described in our culture as the growing to maturity, both mentally and physically; as the period of transition between adulthood and childhood; as a period of significant patterned change; and as a culturally determined problem age (Horrocks, 1962). It has been defined in terms of developmental tasks and in terms of the establishment of ego identity. Erikson (1950) calls the adolescent mind essentially a mind of moratorium, a psychosocial stage between childhood and adulthood and between the morality learned by the child and the ethics to be developed by the adult. Friedenberg (1959) sees adolescence in our society disappearing as the period in which the individual can achieve an articulation of the self. He uses the distresses imposed upon adolescents by society as a commentary on the pathology of society itself. Coleman (1961), in typical sociological fashion, describes the adolescent society from the framework of its social processes. Douvan and Adelson (1966) researched the adolescent experience through the interview and provide dramatic insight into this period of confusion. The school counselor must be familiar with a number of viewpoints concerning adolescence. He should be able to evaluate the meaning of the educational experience within the broader framework but must recognize the impact of both the specific in-school and out-of-school experiences as well.

### Developmental Tasks

Havighurst (1953) describes the following developmental tasks as those associated with the adolescent period.

1. Achieving new and more mature relations with age-mates of both sexes
2. Achieving a masculine or feminine social role
3. Accepting one's physique and using the body effectively
4. Achieving emotional independence of parents and other adults
5. Achieving assurance of economic independence
6. Selecting and preparing for an occupation
7. Preparing for marriage and family life
8. Developing intellectual skills and concepts necessary for civic competence
9. Desiring and achieving socially responsible behavior
10. Acquiring a set of values and an ethical system as a guide to behavior

Obviously, these developmental tasks reflect social and cultural values. They describe the kinds of behavior required to function effectively in our society. Thus, they dictate the most efficacious expenditure of energies of the student, whether or not the student himself is so inclined. The age of adolescence is determined as early adolescence, from thirteen to sixteen, and late adolescence, from seventeen to twenty-one. Obviously these tasks will not hold for every individual at these ages, nor will they apply to every subcultural setting. As socially based requirements, subcultural differences may demand other expectations of the adolescent. Recent concern with the culturally deprived has brought about increased investigation into the dynamics of growth among the disadvantaged. Implications are that considerable variation does exist within our society. The school must therefore recognize the extent to which it reflects and demands basic social behaviors at the expense of ignoring subcultural variations.

It is particularly important that those charged with the development of the broad educational program and those who operate sub-systems be aware of the encapsulated nature of the school milieu. For example, one of the most vital developmental tasks is for the adolescent to achieve a masculine or feminine social role. Provision of exploratory experiences exclusively within the school setting will not suffice to provide realistic understanding of the same sex roles as they are defined in the adult society. As a single example, competition between the boy and girl may well be accepted in the school setting but be subtly out of place in the adult world of work. A highly feminine girl may well maintain femininity within a science or math class but be out of place in engineering. Thus, the school counselor uses his knowledge to insure realistic explorations in settings outside the school as well as within. In each stated developmental task, the school must be perceived as a useful though limited experience both in time and in scope of life events.

### Adolescent Identity

As the primary agent of socialization, the school must provide the adolescent with the opportunity to achieve a healthy personality. The healthy personality has been described as one which actively masters his environment, shows a unity of personality, and perceives the world and himself correctly. Variations of this description would all incorporate to some extent these characteristics. Erikson's (1950) work on growth and crises of the healthy personality has served as the basis for many of the current considerations of personality. Within his epigenetic diagram he presents the adolescent crisis as one of identity versus identity diffusion. He contends that without a sense of ego identity there is no sense of being alive. The adolescent faces the difficult task of achieving from the gradual integration of all identifications a sense of ego identity. Essentially this is achieved through whole-hearted and consistent recognition by the individual of his real accomplishment. He must sense achievement that has meaning in their culture.

The school, then, must provide for these kinds of achievement in individual ways. An adolescent should be provided with the opportunity to master his environment in his own unique way. This often calls for individualization of standardization in an institution. The adolescent must contend with a number of conflicting social presses. He is expected to be several individuals within different settings and to respond differently to various persons.

Efforts of the guidance program should lead toward establishing significant individual contacts for adolescents with adults. The school counselor himself can provide these as well as organize for other similar kinds of experiences among the staff. He can further interpret the often disturbing defensive behavior of the adolescent to others as simply a means to protect oneself from identity diffusion. The school counselor's role in the development of the adolescent identity can be a vital one if he clearly understands his role in assisting youth to understand and cope with these forces.

### The Adolescent Experience

Douvan and Adelson (1966) provide extremely valuable insights into the dynamics of the adolescent experience. They describe a basic future orientation as a distinguishing feature of youngsters making adequate adaptations. A faulty time perspective is associated with measures of ego weakness or lack of personal integration. They identify several interesting differences between the adolescent experience of boys and that of girls. Boys tend to concentrate on the vocational future, concretely crystallized and tied to reality. They are realistically aspiring toward mobility. They appear motivated toward independence, yet show a strong allegiance to the group. Where boys do not reveal these characteristics, there appears to be a tendency toward some personal maladjustment.

Girls, on the other hand, focus on the interpersonal aspects of future life and tend to have less concrete ideas than boys. They seem to bridge the future with more fantasy and to anchor their vocational concepts in terms of adult femininity. Since a girl's mobility aspirations are less formed, she need not test these against her talent and skills. As in the case of boys, those girls who do not reveal these characteristics, particularly a feminine view of the future, appear to be the more troubled adolescents. Girls tend to be more attracted to close two-person friendships, and their concepts about friendship and intimacy are more highly developed than those of boys. It was found that inter-personal development is the best predictor of ego integration.

The effects of the family pattern on the adolescents were reportedly strong and consistent. The democratic families developed adolescents who were unusually self-reliant, poised, effective, and open to criti-cizing and disagreeing. In the authoritarian families, adolescents are apparently compliant but beneath the surface rebellious and impulsive. Across the United States there appears to be a homogeneity of adoles-cent culture that transcends regional and social class lines along the dimensions studied. The basic implication for the school counselor appears to be that with regard to the psycho-social elements of adoles-cence, particular attention must be paid to the differences between boys and girls.

### The Adolescent Society

A description of the adolescent society would logically proceed from an examination of society in general and the place of the youth culture with it. Parsons (1962) provides such an examination and concludes that as a result of the current American society, youth cul-ture today would be expected to manifest signs of internal conflict and would incorporate elements of both conformity and alienation and revolt. He contends that the youth culture today attempts to balance its need for conforming to the expectations of the immediate adult agencies with some kind of outlet for tension and revolt and some sensitivity to the setting beyond the local situation. Thus, he main-tains, the youth culture turns to the peer group with a compulsive in-dependence in relation to certain adult expectations and a compulsive conformity, loyalty, and insistence on liberal observation of its own norms. Except for the lower socioeconomic youth, Parsons contends that youth today are well aware of the value of education in our society and react more positively to it. On the other hand, he feels that edu-cation has the effect of segregating an increasing proportion of the younger age group from the interaction of the broader society. He summarizes the youth culture by saying that its basic orientation seems to be an eagerness to learn, to accept high orders of responsibility, and to fit into society in a more meaningful way. They will not be the "silent generation" of the fifties.

Leading from the general description of the youth culture, Coleman's (1961) popular study of the adolescent society gives even more spe-cific direction for the use of sociological interpretations of the be-havior of the adolescent in the school setting. He reveals the reward system of the adolescent within the context of the school and the models toward which he turns in forming his own behavioral images. He found that the athlete and most popular boy and the best dressed and most popular girl represented the kind of person to be emulated, while the best student did not represent an ideal role model. The implications of Coleman's findings bear directly upon the school setting.

The potential of the school for serving as an effective influence on adolescent behavior has been indicated in both Parsons' general considerations and Coleman's more specific investigations. It remains for the educators themselves to design and implement both social and educational experiences which promote the development of the optimum individual and social characteristics. Many of these planned experiences will fall directly under the auspices of the guidance program through vocational development and educational planning as well as social adjustment. Individual and group procedures hold much promise for such activities. Supportive guidance services can be provided for those activities which are conducted by the teaching staff.

### Socialization

The adolescent must be assisted in meeting the crises of developmental tasks, aided toward accomplishing an identity, and in other ways helped to undergo fruitfully his adolescent experience. Essentially the school will provide for these opportunities. However, it will also serve a social function in the process. In it the student will learn how to be an American. In harmony with other socializers the school transmits the social norms and values of society and the techniques for learning this Americanization process.

Goslin (1965) lists the ways in which this socialization process occurs in the school. These include (1) the transmission of culture through direct teaching, (2) the establishment of social groups in which social skills are acquired, (3) the provision of significant others who serve as supplementary adult role models, and (4) the use of negative and positive sanctions to reinforce acceptable behavior. Some sociologists minimize the formal teaching efforts of the school personnel in accomplishing this socializing process. They contend that the students themselves carry on this process within a structure that is maintained by the staff. They point to the conflict between the peer group and the society in general and see the school's function in this conflict as one of clarifying rather than mediating. Nordstrom, Friedenberg and Gold (1967), for example, place great emphasis upon the social attitudes acquired by students as a result of their school experiences and the effect of these attitudes upon the development of a forceful and strong character.

The school counselor, it would seem, will find himself in the most precarious position of any staff member in this process of socialization. Where conflict occurs between student and school, he will be pressured to take a stand by both sides. He will often have to choose between the role of mediator and clarifier and that of champion or supporter.

Counselor training must provide on-the-job experience for the counselor in identifying and clarifying his own personal position regarding his role in the socializing process. It will not suffice for the school counselor to perform the same institutional functions that he did as a teacher. Basically, it would appear that the profession itself has defined the school counselor's position as that of mediator, facilitator, and supporter of the student where needed. The school counselor clarifies the student's position both to him and to the staff; helps plan meaningful experiences for social and individual growth; and insures the optimum setting for the intellectual growth of the student. Each counselor should be able to perceive the implications of his services in terms of the socializing process.

### The Adolescent as a Student

If we perceive a youth as an adolescent, we will treat him with whatever regard we afford adolescents and expect him to behave accordingly. He usually will. If we perceive a youth as a student, we will teach him or assume that someone else will. If we see him as a bright student, we will probably act differently toward him than if we see him as a dull student. Again, he will usually respond accordingly. On an individual basis this interrelationship of perception-behavior does not have an overly significant impact upon the youth. When it is institutionalized, however, the outcome is far more intense. Students are perceived as bright or dull, college preparatory or vocational, over-achievers or under-achievers, or successes or failures. They even perceive themselves and one another in the same way. Programs are then organized to treat students on the basis of their prefixes, and the school continues to operate efficiently doing whatever needs to be done to the prefixed student.

Such a circumstance is inevitable and not altogether harmful. However, there should be no ignoring of the fact that it exists. The school counselor must often supply or interpret data which categorizes the student. He is referred these same students on the basis of these categories and is expected to treat the category rather than the whole student. The popular categories are usually those which (1) create problems for the efficiency of the school, (2) are demonstrated problems for the student, (3) identify a potential resource for society, (4) identify a potential resource for the student, (5) represent a potential customer for an existing program or funds, (6) are historical, and (7) meet any other of a longer list of such qualifications. Several of these categories are presented here with some implications for the school counselor as he establishes his guidance services. Others are common and should receive as much attention on the part of the counselor.

### The Gifted Student

The presence of giftedness is in part determined by the availability of measures to identify giftedness. In practice, it is also highly dependent upon the existence of specialized programs or resources to cope with or to cultivate the trait. Giftedness in the school setting usually refers to the academically talented, since almost all measures currently used in school settings are measures of or are highly related to scholastic aptitude and most programs for developing giftedness are academic. With the increased energy devoted to the development of science and mathematics, giftedness in these areas is more recently being identified, and programs which nurture the scientifically gifted are in vogue. Athletic giftedness has its own unique set of rewards in both secondary school and in college. Art, music, English, foreign language, and other areas are more likely to go unnoticed unless an enthusiastic, ambitious teacher becomes involved with finding these talents. This condition reflects social press, however, rather than psychological or physiological fact.

The school counselor should organize his guidance services to systematically identify all kinds of giftedness, nurture these talents, and promote programs of further development. Kough and De Hann (1956) identify at least ten kinds of talent which can be nurtured within the school setting: intellectual ability, scientific ability, leadership ability, creative ability, artistic talent, writing talent, musical talent, dramatic talent, mechanical skills, and physical skills. They suggest both selective and extensive all-school and classroom programs to utilize techniques for identifying and assisting the students. Currently available appraisal tools should be utilized and new means of identification explored. Human resources in the form of teachers and community personnel should be encouraged to become involved with the gifted in various ways and available local, state, and federal funds surveyed for establishing programs for the development of talent of all kinds. In brief, the school counselor should have an expanded concept of giftedness to include heretofore ignored areas. He should build into the school program systematic utilization of funds and resources for identifying the talented and in other ways make the guidance program a facilitator in this phase of curriculum development. He should also provide direct special assistance.

## The Creative Student

As intelligence is measured by intelligence tests, it is not necessary that a person be outstanding in intelligence to be recognized as highly creative (MacKinnon, 1966). Research has shown that although most highly creative students are above average in intelligence, current measures of intelligence cannot be used alone to identify potentially highly creative youth (Getzels and Jackson, 1962). There is also considerable evidence that the creative student does not find the ordinary secondary school classroom a hospitable setting. Often his natural make-up causes both him and the teacher difficulty in just the ordinary everyday classroom activities. Yet creativity is one of our most valued characteristics. Almost by definition the creative person exemplifies those traits associated with optimum personality development (Maslow, 1954). Thus, the counselor should be aware of the characteristics of the creative student, ways to measure creativity, and blocks to creative development. He should have a basic understanding of what constitutes a creativity-producing atmosphere.

1. *Characteristics of the creative student.* Torrance (1966) contributes to the growing evidence regarding characteristics of the creative individual with his discussion of personality attributes of divergent thinkers. He describes them as follows.

1. They are always puzzled about something and are seeking answers.
2. They attempt difficult and dangerous tasks, are willing to take risks.
3. They become absorbed in their thinking.
4. They are honest.
5. They may appear to lack consideration for others.
6. They are more shy and more bold. They are timid in social relations and bold in ideas.
7. They are more cultivated and more primitive.
8. They are more destructive and more constructive.
9. They are both madder and saner.
10. They possess a strong sense of humor.
11. They are playful, emotional, adventurous, affectionate and spirited in disagreement.
12. They appear haughty and self-satisfied, but the reverse is true.
13. They are unwilling to accept the judgment of authorities.
14. They like to work alone and strive for distant goals.

2. *Blocks to creativity.* The cultural and social blocks to creativity and divergent thinking are not limited to the school alone. An objective description of the American culture reveals a number of inhibiting

characteristics. Torrance (1965) discusses these social and cultural conditions, which affect divergent thinking as well as problems in maintaining creativity.

He lists the problems in maintaining creativity as (1) the success orientation of our society which eliminates frustration and failure as an acceptable fact of life, (2) a peer orientation wherein children strive toward peer acceptance and peer conformity, (3) the sanctions against questioning and exploration, particularly in the classroom, (4) the over-emphasized or misplaced emphasis upon sex roles and the socially described masculine or feminine proscription of creative traits, (5) the equation of divergency with abnormality, and (6) the work-play dichotomy where one is to enjoy play and dislike work.

3. *Creative teaching.* The counselor would find an examination of the kinds of teaching which promote creativity highly productive not only because of their implications for the creative student, but also because these teaching practices represent basic procedures for any teacher-learner interaction. He can thus take account of classroom climate and the anticipated learning difficulties or productivities which accrue. This insight can be used in working with the student or in co-operating in in-service education for teaching procedure (Torrance, 1966).

### The Culturally Disadvantaged Student

There can be no denying the national emergency resulting from the long-endured condition of social and cultural deprivation suffered by a large segment of our population. Massive programs to rectify this social imbalance have proven to be far short of the need. In some instances the adult generation has already been considered lost for purposes of rehabilitation. The youth are being given a slightly better chance, and it is only with the very youngest children that any real hope can be offered those who have long suffered from social blight. In most instances the secondary school has not had the opportunity to provide assistance for those most seriously affected; they drop out at the earliest possible age. It is quite clear, however, that even where the school has had an opportunity to serve as an agent of change for both individuals and sub-cultures, it has not met the challenge. It is also quite clear that entirely new concepts of education and guidance are needed and that a new kind of teacher and school counselor is called for.

Generally the life conditions of the low-income group are represented by limited alternatives, helplessness, deprivation, and insecurity. Their alienation from society is expressed through their feelings of powerlessness, meaninglessness, anomia, and isolation. They appear to be guided by four distinctive themes: fatalism, an orientation to the present, strong authoritarian interpersonal relationships, and concreteness or pragmatism (Irelan, 1966). Not all school counselors may grasp the significance of the above conditions when translated into human despair. There appears to be an acute need for those who do and choose to work with the youth who must survive in this kind of society. The life of poverty is a self-perpetuating existence for some 34 million Americans, about 16 million of whom are school children. Obviously, guidance can only play a sub-role in a much broader educational effort.

Riessman (1966) provides some hints as to what works with disadvantaged youth from his description of the vastly different personalities who appear to be successful teachers in the classroom. The "boomer" lays down the law, establishes rules, and has learned to use aggressiveness effectively in a classroom. The "maverick" uses fresh and sometimes disturbing ideas to stir and develop a close link to students. The "coach" in his own informal, concrete, physically expressive way shows and teaches by doing. The "quiet" one is sincere, calm, and dignified in his commanding of respect and attention. The "entertainer" actively involves children in a colorful way and has fun with them; he shows students that they count as much as he. The "secular" type is relaxed and informal and is deeply involved in language, its development, and power. No similar description of counseling styles seems to be available. However, the school counselor who chooses to work with the disadvantaged can take his cues from the above. There appears to be much room among the successful for individuality. Involvement seems to be the key.

### The Dropout

Unless a student can be convinced that he should remain in school, the school is obviously limited in the ways in which it can help him. Estimates of the number of students who will drop out of high school in the 1960's appear to be about 7.5 million. Matika and Scheer (1962) estimate that about one-third of the nation's youth will join the adult population without receiving a high school diploma. Yet no more than five percent of the available job facilities will be of the unskilled variety. From 1949, when the first major contribution to literature on the dropout was made by the National Child Labor Committee (Dillon, 1944), until the present, research and conjecture concerning early school leavers has abounded. Some of the literature is contradictory, partly because of the frame of reference used to discuss or research the problem.

A survey of some twenty-two significant research studies on the dropout provides valuable insight into characteristics of the dropout and some general programs for prevention and remediation (Brizendine, 1963). The typical dropout is an older student who has experienced failure in his school work. He dislikes his teachers, his subjects, and school. He comes from a lower-middle or lower socioeconomic family which views school either negatively or indifferently. He does not participate in school activities and feels as though other students are able to get better grades with less work. He sees himself in a job earning money and has developed an image of himself as a dropout. He may not be a chronic disciplinary problem, but his attendance rate is low. The dropout might be either a boy or a girl.

Successful programs of remediation appear to be those which include counseling; curriculum revision to include ability grouping, reading programs, work-study programs, and vocational high school; extra-curricular reforms; and cooperative planning. If the school attempts to provide a program of remediation, it should include adult education for evening school, job upgrading, and counseling. A guidance program often holds the key to the early identification and coordination of efforts to prevent or remediate the school dropout.

# 4

.....................

# The School Counselor

Historically, counseling and guidance have taken place in a number of settings in the United States: in employment centers, hospitals and rehabilitation centers, community agencies, schools, and colleges and universities. Innumerable adjectives have been and are currently being used to preface "counselor" and delineate the extent and focus of the counseling function: vocational, employment, guidance, counseling psychologist, rehabilitation, and school. In discussing the use of the term school "counselor," Super (1964) states that it is the logical derivation of the work of the vocational counselor in the school. He implies that the school counselor is and always has been a vocational counselor and ought to consider himself one. It is true that vocational counseling today, through the significant efforts of vocational development theorists, can proceed from a much broader base than was conceived at the time of Parsons or Brewer. However, there does not yet appear to be a consensus of opinion to encompass the work of the school counselor completely within the functions of the vocational counselor, even with these expanded concepts.

Who, then, is the school counselor, and what are his characteristics? How is he selected? What is the nature of his training? What does he do? What is his future?

## The School Counselor as a Person

There seems to be considerable conjecture as to what kinds of persons make effective school counselors. Wrenn (1962) sees the counselor as the most important single factor in counseling. He suggests that the counselor needs to be one who understands himself psychologically, one who can control his biases and defenses. He needs to be socially sensitive and flexible, imaginative, and in control of his emotions. He points out that these characteristics usually take a lifetime to develop and then are usually accomplished through some professional assistance.

A number of school counselor characteristics can be implied from the ASCA Proposed Statement of Policy for Secondary School Counselors and the Proposed Guidelines for the Implementation of Policy (1964). Therein the counselor is seen as a person who accepts the responsibility of involving himself in the lives of pupils. He would be a philosophical eclectic. He recognizes his own values and needs and is striving to distinguish them from those of others, particularly students. Since the report is primarily an attempt to define the professional functioning of the school counselor, personal characteristics are not treated directly as such.

The APGA Standards for the Preparation of School Counselors (1964) suggest that the effective school counselor would have six basic qualities that are particularly important. He believes in the inherent worth of each individual; he has a commitment to individual human values; he is alert to the world; he has the quality of open-mindedness with a wide range of interests, attitudes, and beliefs; he has an understanding of himself and the ways his feelings and values can affect his work; and he feels a commitment to counseling as a profession.

Reports of studies of the characteristics of practicing counselors continue to flow out of college campuses and secondary school settings into the most popular professional journals: *The Personnel and Guidance Journal, The Journal of Counseling Psychology, The School Counselor,* and *The Journal of Counselor Education and Supervision.* Summaries of these studies are reported every three years in capsule form in the *Review of Educational Research.* To present them in organized fashion would be nearly impossible, for to date there has been no framework for evaluating the conceptualizations of the research itself.

Roeber (1963) presents a sense of much of the research which attempted to identify characteristics of the successful counselor. He found studies conducted on attitudes, interests, motivation, multifactor personality assessment, tolerance for ambiguity, and values. As he points out, "Research has not been effective thus far in isolating selection criteria which consistently distinguish between successful and unsuccessful counselors."

Fullmer and Bernard (1964) recognize, as do most others, that the counselor who met all criteria would be a paragon. They point out, however, that it would be more profitable to view these characteristics as goals. Training programs could then examine potential counselors not only for existing characteristics but for the potential for developing these characteristics. Such an approach would also have implications for the development of the training program itself. They suggest that a counselor should be able to develop inter-personal skills through his training, should be a growing person, should be acceptant of others, and should be willing to become involved. He should have the capacity for research, a sense of humor, openness towards oneself and others, and the ability to become aware of and involved in process.

While at one time there seemed to be an issue regarding whether or not the counselor himself should have to undergo counseling, in practice this seems to have been resolved in practice in favor of the negative. Undoubtedly this is partly because of the lack of adequate services in most training programs for providing for counseling or analysis. In somewhat the same vein, it is generally recognized that the current mental health of the counselor or other helping person is to be judged not so much on the absence or presence of his own personal problems as on the way these problems are being met in daily lives.

In general, then, a number of problems exist in describing the characteristics of the school counselor. First, the complete school counselor role includes a number of activities best performed and of interest to persons of different traits. Second, success in the training program may require characteristics different from and incompatible with those called for in the performance of school counseling. Third, a valid definition of, much less the means to identify, certain espoused ideal characteristics has not yet been satisfactorily accomplished. Fourth, as in any other occupation, job success may be differentially determined according to peers, performance, principal, and perceptions of self. Finally, there exists the problem of describing who *is* the school counselor as well as who *should* be a school counselor.

With no conclusive evidence to the contrary presently available, it would seem that school counseling is similar to many other occupations in that it can be effectively conducted by a number of kinds of persons and that many kinds of persons can find it a rewarding experience. However, with specific school counselor roles (counseling, for example), there seems to be growing evidence of some of the characteristics necessary. Most counselor educators feel they know what makes a good counselor, particularly those counselor educators who occupy themselves with direct, close involvement with trainees in practicum settings. As Tyler (1961) suggests, this is probably the person who can permit rich and deep relationships with other human beings to develop.

## Selection of the School Counselor

In light of the current lack of definitive criteria for identifying the successful school counselor, one might ask about the means of selection of school counselors. Selection refers essentially to three distinct processes, each dependent upon the other but not necessarily conducted in complete awareness one with the others. These are the self-selection of the counselor candidate himself, the selection by the counselor training program for potential counselor trainees, and the selection or employment of the counselor by the school administrator.

### Self-selection of School Counselors

The question of who chooses to become a school counselor has been treated by a number of counselor educators over the past ten years. At one time there appeared to be a serious issue raised as to whether the school counselor should come primarily from the ranks of teachers. This appears to have been resolved with the general consensus being that he should. In part this was due to the prevalent certification requirements of having to possess a teaching certificate and in part because of the current practice of recruiting counselors from the teaching ranks. Since, however, there has never been any major attempt at providing conclusive evidence of the necessity of teaching experience for becoming an effective school counselor, it can only be surmised that the issue was resolved on some basis other than that of competence. Undoubtedly, maintenance of the status quo was one factor; the political aspects of the psychologist-educator roles in counselor education was the other major factor.

Studies of the teaching background for secondary school counselors reveal that education leads the list of undergraduate majors (Riccio and Weathersby, 1964). The subject areas in education from which most counselors come are social studies, English, science, and physical education. Obviously, this is due in part to the larger numbers of teachers in those areas; however, there does seem to be a proportionately greater percentage of secondary school counselors with the social studies background. If one assumes a compatibility of interests between the teaching field and school counseling, it is possible to see why social studies teachers could find school counseling compatible. As research with the Strong Vocational Interest Blank has indicated, social studies teachers are more nearly like other social service workers in their interest patterns than they are like math teachers. Interests of math teachers, on the other hand, correlate higher with those of carpenters and printers than they do with social studies teachers.

It would be folly to assume, however, that interest alone is the only motivation for the teacher who goes into counseling. Salary increment, the availability of NDEA funds for graduate work, job flexibility and mobility, and the greater status afforded the school counselor in some schools are all factors which lead teachers into counseling. With regard to the latter, however, the school counselor often finds, as he moves from the teaching ranks to those of the pupil-personnel workers and counseling and guidance in general, that he has not improved his relative status position within his new field. In the same light, if one considers that interests are generally dichotomous and that interest patterns evolve from rejections as much, if not more than from attractions, it is not inconceivable that a large number of guidance personnel have moved *from* teaching rather than *to* guidance.

NDEA Counseling and Guidance Institute enrollees often reveal that at least one primary motivator of those attending was the opportunity to leave the classroom. This is even more obvious with those who have committed themselves to a training program without any clearly conceptualized idea of what the counseling function involves. Generally, this represents an attempt to interact with students in more close personal contact than is allowed the classroom teacher. Vocational autobiographies of school counselors are also extremely revealing. It is not uncommon to find many counselors in counselor education programs who are generally in the exploratory stage in their own vocational development. Indeed, if counseling does differ from teaching, then the counselor who moves into guidance work from teaching is a vocational adolescent.

It would appear that the self-selection of counselors will continue to include those who have performed successfully in teaching. Successful teaching experience, however, need not always be used as a screen criterion in every case. The forward looking counselor education program will include provisions for self-exploration experiences early in training as well as task-exploration for the counselor candidate. Such provisions should allow for the greatest number of potential candidates to investigate the field of school counseling while at the same time minimizing the waste of time and effort.

### Selection for Counselor Education

Selection procedures for counselor education programs vary among institutions from open admission, or selective retention, to a strict admissions procedure. Optimally there would be cooperation between the school administrator and counselor educator in determining the essentials of both job performance and preparational program require-ment. This cooperation would extend beyond placement of the coun-selor into the satisfactory performance of his tasks. The ASCA report reflects this thinking with the statement that:

> School counselor education does not terminate with the completion of a formal program, but continues throughout the career of the coun-selor. Therefore, counselors have a responsibility to plan, implement, and participate in in-service and other post-certification programs and study designed to maintain and promote professional competency. (ASCA, 1964)

Regarding selection by the counselor training program, the APGA Committee on Professional Preparation and Role calls for efficient procedures of selective admission and selective retention. This would include the accumulation of evidence of personal qualifications for counseling as well as the ability to master academic requirements. Procedures and standards for selection would be expected to demon-strate flexibility and continued evaluation. Endorsement by the faculty would indicate the counselor candidate to be competent at the level for which he was prepared. The Standards for Counselor Education in the Preparation of Secondary School Counselors accepts these bases and goes on to call for a placement service as well as a program of research designed to evaluate selection, retention, endorsement, and placement.

Hill (1965) recommends that school counselors become more in-volved with the identification of potential counselors and that school administrators work through their local pupil personnel and guidance committees in their plans to recruit prospective school counselors. He also calls for closer coordination between school systems and univer-sities in both the selection and placing of counselors. Follow-up service through visitation and consultation is called for, and he feels that conferences between practicing school counselors and counselors in training would be helpful.

It would appear, then, that promising strides are being made by both counselor educators and the professional organization of school counselors to come to grips with the problem of selection and reten-tion procedures. Until the institutions themselves, however, put into effect those guidelines which would make selection more professional, differences will still exist among institutions in these practices. In some instances, to fully implement some of the suggestions would involve revamping to some degree the training program itself. Earlier prac-ticum experiences, staff involvement in decisions to retain students, and concentrated individualized experiences for areas of need would be the minimum kinds of considerations necessary. With the current emphasis being given to self-evaluations by counselor education programs, the future holds more promise that such changes will occur than at any time in the past.

### Selection by School Administrators

Selection procedures by school administrators in employing school counselors vary perhaps to an even greater extent than selection by the counselor training program. A list of these procedures would include the following, some of which would comprise the steps expected in a given school system for hiring a school counselor.

1. The prospective counselor would make his interest known to the proper personnel, usually the Director of Guidance and Counseling and an administrator.

2. He would present evidence of certification or an agreement of intent to become certified.

3. He would complete an application form requesting his background data. This would usually include his educational background, his work experience, both teaching and non-teaching, and evidence of some personal qualifications. In lieu of an application form he may be requested to develop a resume of training and experiences.

4. He would take a battery of tests, generally under outside supervision. These might include any of the following:

Interest Inventory
Teacher Attitude Inventory
Comprehensive Guidance Test
Group Personality Inventory
Projective Personality Test
Individual Intelligence Test
Scholastic Aptitude Test

5. He would be interviewed by a committee representing the guidance and counseling specialists, administrators, teachers, and outside consultants. This would result in an initial evaluation.

6. He would attend a workshop or seminar for orientation to the guidance services in the local school system and for further evaluation.

7. He would apprise himself of openings for guidance and counseling positions as they occur and are announced.

8. He would make formal application for an announced opening.

9. He would participate in observation-participation activities on the job after he has been considered for a position.

10. He would serve a period of temporary assignment pending a full appointment.

11. He would cooperate in follow-up evaluations and take part in in-service training throughout his tenure.

Obviously not all school administrators would find it possible to implement all of these steps in their employment procedures, nor would some feel it necessary to do so. The real bases for selecting one applicant over another will not in many instances ever be fully revealed. However, procedures which include judgments and recommendations by school counselors themselves as well as counselor educators would be far superior to those made by administrators alone. With the current diversity of function within the school counselor role, it is essential that placement in a position not be considered completed before a counselor has had an opportunity to implement his skills and techniques in the setting where they can be used to the best advantage. Some counselors can function more effectively in certain schools than they can in others. Some can perform specific counselor duties better than they can others. Thus, the employment procedure should continue until the counselor is placed in the position in which his talents are best utilized and in which he feels most comfortable. An attitude of flexibility and growth should permeate both the administrator's and the counselor's approach to job placement.

### Certification of the School Counselor

The situation regarding state certification of school counselors is a rapidly changing one and is apparently highly charged with feelings of concern. From 1926, when New York became the first state to require certification to the present, nearly all states have or will have this requirement in the immediate future. The proliferation of patterns among states has resulted in comparisons and charges of inadequacies even where certification is required. Wrenn (1962), Hill (1965), Byrne (1963), Roeber (1963), and Zeran and Riccio (1962) each have examined the current status of certification and conclude that much yet needs to be done for improvement. The school counselor, the counselor educator, the state department supervisor, the school administrator, and even the college administrator who hires the counselor educator are all called upon to bring order and legitimacy to the intent of certification plans.

Current plans provide for both provisional certificates and standard professional certificates in most states. Almost all require teaching experience. In most states it is possible to become certified without the recommendation or endorsement of counselor preparation from the institution and thus be employed as an effective counselor on the basis of minimum performance in courses of study. Areas of counselor preparation required in certification plans generally include the following:

(1) Philosophy and Principles of Guidance, (2) Methods of Studying Individuals, (3) Collection, Evaluation, and Use of Occupational and Other Types of Information, (4) Counseling Theory and Techniques, and, to a lesser extent, (5) Growth and Development of Individuals, (6) Administrative and Community Relationships, (7) Group Work Theory and Techniques, (8) Supervised Experience in Counseling, and (9) Research and Evaluation.

Most significant for counselor education programs are the ACES standards (1962) currently being examined and tested in counselor education programs throughout the country. Consideration is given in the standards to the philosophy and objectives of the program; the curriculum; selection, retention, endorsement, and placement; and administrative relationships and institutional resources. Specific to the program of studies, the following are recommended.

a. The foundations and dynamics of human behavior and of the individual in his culture.
b. The educational enterprise and processes of education.
c. Professional studies in school counseling and related guidance activities:
   (1) philosophy and principles underlying guidance and other pupil personnel services;
   (2) individual appraisal, including the nature and range of human characteristics and methods of measuring them;
   (3) vocational development theory; informational materials and services;
   (4) counseling theory and practice;
   (5) statistics and research methodology, independent research, and an introduction to data processing and programming techniques;
   (6) group procedures in counseling and guidance;
   (7) professional relationships and ethics in keeping with the APGA Ethical Standards;
   (8) administration and coordination of guidance and pupil personnel services;
   (9) supervised experience.

## Preparation of the School Counselor

New developments in programs of counselor preparation take place so rapidly that literature concerning this aspect of counselor education is outdated before it reaches print. This circumstance of change is being readily accepted within the profession and, indeed, sought after and planned for. As Zeran and Riccio (1962) state:

The story of counselor education is a saga of change. Partial preparation for part-time counselors is no longer acceptable; counselor preparation is no longer looked upon as the sole responsibility of a single counselor-education department or division; increased emphasis is being placed upon the concept of the counselor as a person; recognition is being given to the place the behavioral and social sciences have in counselor education; and the integration of theory and practice with experiences on three levels is now accepted. Using these as guide-lines, counselor-educators have proceeded to maintain direction amid change and new emphases. (Zeran and Riccio, 1962)

Perhaps the best perspective on the direction of counselor education specifically in regard to its content and related instructional concerns can be gained from four professional statements, each of which needs to be considered as proposals. These are the Wrenn report of 1962, the ASCA report of 1964, the APGA committee report of 1964, and the ACES standards of 1964. Among other matters, each directs itself to the content of programs in the preparation of the school counselor.

The observer can detect a continuity of content throughout all four of these professional statements. There appears to be an agreement regarding the necessary understandings for the adequate performance of the functions of the secondary school counselor. There also appears to be agreement on the need for both didactic and practicum-type learning experiences. Optimally this program would be undertaken by a full-time graduate student; however, realism dictates the continued attendance of part-time prospective counselors in training. Obviously programs which can anticipate full-time students will have an advantage over those which can not. Between concentrated efforts on the part of the professionals to maintain standards of preparation and to meet the demands of realistic counselor trainee circumstances, a sound program of preparation should evolve.

### Informal Preparation

Counseling dynamics are special instances of human behavior. The concepts which guide the counselor in understanding himself and his own behavior may be found in everyday life. Thus the counselor continues his informal education by observing people in those settings in which they function. While he can not maintain the high degree of attentiveness, sensitivity, and openness required in counseling in his daily life, his observations ought to be deliberate and practiced. A school counselor should take every opportunity to sample life in every social strata. He should recognize that the language of the musician and that of the dock worker can tell him much of what he needs to know about people and their strategies for living.

Continued indulgence in art and literature are required of all growing persons. Man's expression of himself occurs not only in the spoken word but in the written word and through non-verbal communication as well. The development of characters in novels provides in capsule form total dimensions of real lives. The outer expression of inner feelings through art is yet another way for people to be read. In the secondary school the counselor should strive toward becoming as familiar with the humanness of art, music, and literature as are his colleagues, the art teacher, the music teacher, and the language arts teacher. No instance of human behavior or of human expression should be beyond the legitimate scope of the school counselor's endeavor to understand. His informal education will continue in conjunction with and far beyond his formal training. Constant application of all he perceives and understands in the daily lives of the students and staff with whom he works should provide the school counselor with the stimulation to grow professionally through living.

### Continuing Education

The formal education of the school counselor should continue beyond his initial employment. This should constitute a formally organized program of in-service education. The content and nature of the learning experiences themselves should be cooperatively developed with counselor educators. They should be directed or at least guided by a counselor educator. Wherever possible, released time should be provided for in-service education for the school counselor. To facilitate such provisions, cooperative in-service programs could be developed with teachers and other staff members as well. Local guidance associations should become involved in group efforts to plan and conduct such programs. Often the counselor finds himself isolated professionally with few others with whom to discuss pertinent matters. Even though he may communicate with his colleagues, the teachers, on educational concerns, there is no doubt that the counselor also needs involvement with those in his own specific professional group. The guidance associations can provide such seminars and forums. To increase their potential for professional growth, currently conducted actvities of this nature should be a part of a cooperative university-public school effort toward continuing education. Credits should be awarded wherever possible; and the impact of such efforts should be visible in the school guidance program.

# 5

# The Objectives and Implementation of Guidance Services

Earlier chapters in this monograph have dealt with the major forces that must be given serious study before one can hope to establish an effective program of guidance services. In addition to these forces in general, however, cognizance must be taken of the fact that the guidance program must function at a given point in space and time. The counselor is not simply a counselor in the abstract; he is a counselor-in-situation. Therefore, as the counselor attempts to put down on paper the objectives he hopes to realize through the establishment of his guidance program, he must take into consideration the sociological and psychological data which distinguish the community in which his school is located from the communities in which all other schools are located. Further, he must state the objectives of the guidance program in such a fashion that at a later point in time the objectives will be susceptible to evaluation. Perhaps the most effective method of stating the objectives of a guidance program is to state them in terms of the behavioral outcomes of students that the guidance program is intended to effect. Bruce Duke, a school counselor in Ohio, has attempted to study the small Ohio community in which he was employed and to establish appropriate objectives for a guidance program in such a community. The results of his efforts are presented here.

## Guidance Objectives in Smalltown High School

The village of Smalltown, Ohio is located at the intersection of state routes A and B, approximately thirty-five miles northwest of a metropolitan area. Smalltown was founded in the early 1800's and during the Civil War period was a minor stop on the Underground Railway. To facilitate a better understanding of the educational system in Smalltown, it is necessary first to describe the population and its employment and educational characteristics.

The national census of 1960 showed the population of Smalltown to be 1,810. A population breakdown shows:

| | | |
|---|---|---|
| White | — | 1,712 |
| Negro | — | 92 |
| Other | — | 6 |

In 1960 there were 563 households in Smalltown, thirty-one of which were non-white. The population as of July, 1965, was 1,862, showing an increase in five years of fifty-two people.

Industry in Smalltown is virtually non-existent. In 1960 eight people were listed as employed by the single industry of the village; however, the industry has since closed its doors.

The majority of workers in Smalltown are employed by industries in the larger cities outside of town. Approximately twenty-five percent of Smalltown's work force own or work on farms. Those who work on farms are generally tenant farmers and mostly Negro.

Smalltown is a slow, very conservative community, untouched by the hustle and bustle of present day society. It seeks no industry; it desires no growth. New ideas are often feared before explanations can be given. To the outsider, Smalltown appears backwards, and perhaps it is. The people of Smalltown, however, find happiness and security in their small community and are highly protective of what they consider "the good life."

Operating within the above setting is the Smalltown School System. The school plant consists of one building, originally constructed in 1908, with several more recent additions. Children within a radius of five to eight miles outside the village proper attend this school.

The system defines elementary school as grades K through six, while the high school consists of grades seven through twelve. As of September, 1966, the elementary school had 597 pupils and the high school had 421 pupils, for a combined enrollment of 1,018. This total includes twelve special education high school students.

The school system has the following administrative personnel: a superintendent of schools, a high school principal, an elementary school principal, a dean of students (whose main function is discipline for all grades), and a school counselor.

The school system employs about thirty-five teachers. At the termination of each academic year twenty to thirty percent of the teachers move on to different systems. Because of this migration of generally younger teachers, there is a core of older teachers who tend to dominate faculty thought. On most issues the faculty reflects the conservative attitude expressed by the community as a whole.

The following objectives are based on this writer's perceptions of feasible alternatives for Smalltown, Ohio. Some of these objectives may appear to the reader to be petty in nature, while others might seem quite risky; taken out of the Smalltown situation, this may well be true. However, because they are to be applied to a specific situation, they are quite relevant and contribute to the growth of the students.

1. To assist all students in acquiring an understanding of the nature of the guidance program in Smalltown. This would include an explanation concerning purposes, facilities, and types of help available to students. At present, awareness of guidance and its potential for students is extremely lacking in Smalltown.

2. To assist students in acquiring an understanding of their scholastic aptitudes as they relate to their aspirations. This could be done through a limited testing program (limited due to financial reasons). An individual test interpretation, or group interpretations where applicable, must accompany testing so that the test will become relevant for the student.

3. To help students acquire an adequate concept of self. This objective, in part, grows out of the second objective. As the student gains accurate information about himself (interests, abilities, aptitudes, and attitudes), he can receive greater insight and understanding concerning his actions. Development of an adequate self concept can be facilitated through accurate and frank test interpretations; in this way, objective three is closely related to objective two.

4. To help equip students to become productive members of society upon completion of their high school training. This would include assisting students with college preparation and helping other students with vocational pursuits.

5. To institute, if possible, a vocational training program for selected students, beginning in the junior year. This program would be for the potential drop-out and for those students seeking careers in various trades (plumbers, carpenters, mechanics, etc.). This program would be similar to the Neighborhood Youth Corps

program. Because of the remoteness of the area, a sanctioned Youth Corps program is impossible.

6. To help students, through the developmental nature of guidance, to become more aware of individual freedom and self direction.
7. To help to develop a working relationship with the faculty. This is essential in Smalltown if any programs are to be successful. Perhaps the best method for doing this is simply to help teachers, rather than hinder them, in their relations to their students.

While these objectives are few in number, they represent a monumental task for a counselor in Smalltown. The proper combination of flexibility and perseverance in their application will insure progress.

## Guidance Objectives in a Larger High School

Obviously, the objectives listed above are not comprehensive enough for a guidance program in a large urban high school which has a larger budget, more personnel, and a more diversified student body than Smalltown High School. Jessie Morrison, a doctoral student in guidance and counseling who has had considerable experience as a school counselor, has prepared a list of objectives appropriate for an urban high school. Instead of listing her objectives as general statements, she has listed them in the form of the behavioral outcomes that each of the basic guidance services discussed later in this chapter is intended to produce. Her objectives are listed below.

### Objectives for a Guidance Program at Urban High School

I. Individual Analysis Service:
1. To assist the student in identifying his abilities, aptitudes, and interests.
2. To assist the student in understanding his achievement in relationship to his potential.
3. To assist the student in identifying hobbies, social abilities, and occupational interests in relation to career planning.
4. To assist the student in planning his educational program in school to be consistent with his post-high school plans.
5. To assist the student in identifying problems which interfered with his optimum achievement in his school subjects.

II. Information Service:
1. To develop a broad and realistic view of life's opportunities and problems at all levels of training.
2. To create an awareness of the need and an active desire for accurate and valid occupational, educational, and personal-social information.
3. To promote assistance in narrowing choices progressively to

specific activities which are appropriate to aptitudes and interests.

4. To assist in the mastery of the techniques of obtaining and interpreting information for progressive self-directedness.
5. To assist in the development of tentative educational and occupational plans based upon thorough self-study.
6. To present specific techniques to aid in meeting immediate needs confronting school leavers, such as obtaining employment, continuing an educational program or establishing a home.

III. Counseling Service:

1. To assist the student in understanding, accepting, and utilizing his personality traits.
2. To help the student to recognize his aspirations in relation to his traits and aptitudes.
3. To aid a student in developing his potentials to their optimum.
4. To assist the student in becoming more self-directive.
5. To assist the student in identifying, understanding and solving his problems which hinder his self-development.
6. To assist the student who needs this help in developing a more positive self-concept.

IV. Placement Service:

1. To assist the student in making applications to institutions of higher learning or other programs for post-high school education or training.
2. To assist the student in securing employment that will be satisfactory to him.
3. To assist the student in securing summer or part-time employment where desired.

## Implementing Guidance Services

Once the objectives of the guidance program have been identified, it becomes necessary to implement the specific guidance services which comprise the guidance program. The manner in which these services are to be implemented is largely dependent upon the quality and number of personnel who are available to staff the guidance program. It is important at this point to consider the organizational concerns relevant to the assignment of specific duties to counselors.

### Organizational Patterns of Guidance Programs

As indicated in Chapter 1, guidance services do not just happen; they must be planned. In larger school systems, there is often an assistant superintendent of schools who is given primary responsibility for planning and organizing a system-wide guidance program. But in larger systems the problems confronting selected schools in the system differ widely, and consequently the guidance workers in each school building must concern themselves with the most appropriate means of implementing the broad policies established by the Board of Education and conveyed through the central administration. The focus in this section will be on the kinds of organization that are likely to be found in a total school system. This emphasis is predicated on the belief that it is the things that happen to a counselor daily as he attempts to do his job that make him happy or unhappy, that render him effective or ineffective. Emphasis is therefore placed upon what can be done in a school building in the way of organization to help the counselor do a more effective job.

Before looking at several ways in which the counseling staff might be organized in a given school, it is important to realize that certain principles of organization must be adhered to closely if any organizational pattern is to prove effective. These principles are listed below:

1. Although there is much palaver in the literature about team effort in meeting all tasks, the experience of the authors has been that the principal of the school has more to say about what will be done in a school program than anyone else. The plan of organization adopted in a school building must meet with the approval of the school principal.

2. There must be a definite and demonstrable relationship between the objectives of the guidance program and the pattern of organization of the guidance program.

3. Each guidance worker in the school must have a job description which clearly defines his responsibilities.

4. The guidance worker must have sufficient authority and administrative support to meet his responsibilities.

5. Organizational patterns should be kept as simple and as uncomplicated as possible.

Although a number of people have suggested that there should be one counselor for every 250 students in a school, there are very few schools with such a ratio at this time, and it will undoubtedly be some time before we reach this idealistic and perhaps magical figure. There are probably more than five hundred high school students in this country for every full-time counselor equivalent, a factor which must be taken into consideration in evaluating patterns of counselor organization.

At present, there are five basic ways in which counselors are organized to meet their obligations. Each of these organizational patterns will be discussed below.

1. *Sex.* In many schools, counselors are assigned by sex. That is, there is a counselor for boys and a counselor for girls. This pattern of organization is essentially a carry-over from pre-guidance school days when there was a Dean of Boys and a Dean of Girls. The pattern is predicated on the assumption that members of different sexes have problems that are peculiar and that are best handled by counselors of the same sex. This kind of thinking waned during the heyday of Carl Rogers but is currently receiving more emphasis in a number of school programs, possibly as a result of contemporary concerns over sexual mores among adolescents and perhaps because of the dramatic increase in the number of school girls who are inflicted with venereal disease or are bearing illegitimate offspring. This pattern of organization is generally found in smaller secondary schools.

2. *Rotating Grade-Level.* Another way of organizing counselors in the secondary school is to assign each counselor to one or more grades of students. In this pattern the counselor picks up a grade of students, say at the tenth grade, and becomes the counselor for all tenth grade students. When these students move on to the eleventh grade, this counselor becomes the eleventh grade counselor and later the twelfth grade counselor. The obvious advantage to this pattern of organization is that in many cases the counselor has the same counselees for several years and gets to know each one of them quite well. There are many who maintain that this is the most effective way of organizing counselors in schools today. It is also pointed out that this pattern of organization is student-centered in that it is based on the notion that the counselor who knows his counselees well can probably do a more effective job in working with them. The disadvantage to this approach, however, is that the counselor is expected to become expert at a different set of tasks each year. He must become expert in college admissions work or employment assistance at least once every three years, for example, and he places emphasis on the different developmental tasks confronting his counselees each year.

3. *Stationary Grade-Level.* In this pattern of organization, emphasis is placed upon the counselor becoming expert in a series of tasks related to the grade level at which he counsels. The counselor in this pattern might be labeled a tenth-grade counselor. When one group of tenth-graders moves on to the eleventh-grade, the counselor does not move on with them; he simply picks up another group of tenth-graders.

4. *Function.* One of the more unnoticed consequences of categorical federal aid to education has been the impact of such aid on the pattern of organization of guidance services. It is not uncommon for counselor educators to receive requests for such guidance personnel

as "counselor for college-bound youth," "counselor for disadvantaged youth," "testing officer," and "counselor for vocational education students." In larger guidance programs, this aid has reached such proportions that counselors are assigned titles to indicate the functions they will perform with selected members of the student body. The advantage in assigning counselors by function centers on the conception of the counselor as a specialist in the performance of selected guidance tasks. For example, a counselor who works almost exclusively with college-bound youth can be expected to know the college admissions personnel at colleges and universities attended by students at his school and can have current information about curricular changes, scholarship opportunities, and relevant Federal and state legislation related to college attendance. There is much to be said for the assignment of counselors on the basis of function. In fact, some counselor educators have indicated that it might be desirable for some guidance personnel to do counseling and for others who are not comfortable in the one-to-one relationship to be assigned to such guidance work as test administration and group dissemination of occupational information. In guidance programs in which counselors are assigned by function, it becomes necessary to add staff members in terms of competencies required to complement the specialists currently on the guidance staff. An emphasis in such programs is placed on the counselor as an expert in the performance of selected tasks rather than on the counselor as an effective person prepared to work with all youth on all of their problems.

5. *Function and Grade.* In some guidance programs in which there are five or more counselors, an attempt has been made to combine both the functionalist and stationary grade-level approaches. In such a program, there are counselors for tenth, eleventh, and twelfth graders as well as specialists in vocational and college counseling. The vocational and college counselors, although they do work with a number of individual students, spend a considerable portion of their time in serving in a consultative capacity to the grade-level counselors. The vocational counselor also handles all the testing aspects of the vocational counseling program and is responsible for the placement function of the guidance program for non-college bound students, both for those students who leave school to accept jobs and those who go on to post-high school technical institutes. The vocational counselor also serves as school liaison with such governmental agencies as state employment services, youth opportunity centers, and manpower development and training centers. The college counselor handles all specialized testing programs such as the National Merit Scholarship Program; he visits the campuses most frequently attended by graduates of his high school;

and he is responsible for keeping up-to-date on all legislation (for example, Project Upward Bound), that might help a larger percentage of the school population to secure a college education. The function-and-grade approach makes it possible for the college and vocational counselors to spend a considerable portion of their time outside of the school building engaged in activities that are essential to the welfare of an effective guidance program. As many forces other than the school become interested in developing programs to assist all youth to participate more fully in the American dream, it becomes imperative that school counselors attempt to utilize these agencies more than ever before, for the guidance-relevant programs currently being established by industrial and governmental agencies are in general innovative endeavors to tackle problems which the schools have in the past failed miserably to resolve. The function-and-grade approach makes it possible for the specialist counselors to be outside the school when necessary and desirable and for the generalists to be in the school to meet any problems that should arise. The major difficulty with the function-and-grade-level approach is that "jurisdictional disputes" will arise frequently if the specialists and generalists are not in complete accord on their respective roles and responsibilities. More than any other approach to organizing the tasks of school counselors, this approach demands that detailed job descriptions be provided for all school counselors in the guidance program.

Although the authors believe that the function-and-grade level approach is most relevant to guidance programs in contemporary America, it should be remembered that the approach which is most effective in a given school is the relevant approach for that particular school. It is imperative that school counselors be in considerable agreement as to which of the five approaches listed above is most relevant to a given guidance program. If they are not in agreement, school counselors will devote a disproportionate amount of their time meeting their own needs rather than in attempting to meet the needs of their students.

## Specific Guidance Services

The guidance program is generally comprised of five specific services. These services are called (1) the analysis of the individual service, (2) the information service, (3) the counseling service, (4) the placement service, and (5) evaluation. The first four of these services will be discussed in this chapter. A special chapter is devoted to the evaluation of guidance services. However, before one can begin to discuss the implementation of these services in a guidance program, several questions must be raised and answered.

1. What guidance services are already available in the school? Even in schools which do not have an organized guidance program,

there are often many facets of an organized guidance program in existence. These factors should be identified, organized, and capitalized upon.

2. What kind of guidance competencies are available on the part of current staff members?

3. Who are these people and would they be willing to serve on a committee established to discuss the implementation of the guidance services listed above?

Once these questions have been answered, the person entrusted with the responsibility for establishing a guidance program can begin to establish some kind of priority — with the help of a committee of teachers and possibly representation of the administration — for the introduction of guidance services.

1. *The Analysis of the Individual Service.* This service is an attempt to gather sufficient information on the individual student so that these data might be employed to help the individual student secure as much benefit as possible from the educational experience. The major components of this service are the cumulative record folder and the testing program. Both of these aspects of the guidance program are available in all schools, with or without organized guidance programs.

The cumulative record folder contains a wealth of data on each student. It contains identifying data, health and physical data, psychological data, data on social environment, achievement and activity data, and data on educational and vocational aspirations. All school personnel should be involved in the compilation of these data. And all school personnel should make use of these data. Since all schools undoubtedly have cumulative record folders, there is no need to undertake a discussion of these records. Any reader interested in learning more about cumulative record folders should consult any standard text on the techniques of guidance.

The second major component of the analysis of the individual service is the testing program. Tests serve many purposes. They are useful for discovering exceptional pupils, the slow learner, and the gifted; for appraising a pupil's chance of success in a college or at a particular occupational level; for identifying a pupil's special abilities; for diagnosing his disabilities in learning, for appraising his progress; and for comparing his present performance with that of other pupils or with his own past performances.

Tests are available to high-school counselors for judging mechanical, clerical, musical, and art aptitudes and for measuring aptitude in particular school subjects and in some occupations. Like tests of general intelligence, however, these tests show what a student can do rather than what he will do. Consequently, the counselor must also know the pupil's personality characteristics, which indicate to some extent how well he may use his abilities.

To study the pupil's personality, the counselor will rely less upon test techniques than upon such procedures as descriptive ratings, personal and teacher observations, anecdotal records, the case study, and most important, a synthesis of data from a number of sources.

The use of vocational aptitude tests and interest inventories is limited by the fact that they can give only a general indication of the occupations in which a counselee may succeed. School personnel use these instruments because they are useful, interesting aids in dealing with immediate problems of adjustment.

Achievement tests are used to determine the progress of students in their achievement of skills and knowledge. The better standardized achievement tests tend to measure the student's capacity to use what he has learned in a variety of situations, rather than strictly to measure the retention of subject matter.

Meaningful interpretation is the most important part of testing, for without it tests are of little value. It is just as important to know why a student is where he is as it is to know where a student is, and it is through test analysis and follow-up conferences that testing results are of use in guidance. The results of most tests and inventories should be interpreted to each individual so that he will be able to understand himself better.

Two principles seem to provide a sound basis for communicating the information obtained from testing. The two principles are absolutely interdependent: without the second the first is empty, and without the first the second is pointless.

The first: PARENTS HAVE THE RIGHT TO KNOW WHATEVER THE SCHOOL KNOWS ABOUT THE ABILITIES, PERFORMANCE, AND PROBLEMS OF THEIR CHILDREN.

The second: THE SCHOOL HAS THE OBLIGATION TO COMMUNICATE UNDERSTANDABLE AND USABLE KNOWLEDGE TO PARENTS.

Whether by written report or by individual conference, the school must make sure it is giving real information rather than merely the illusion of information that bare numbers or canned interpretations often afford. The information must be presented in terms that parents can absorb and use.

It must be recognized at all times that tests are only tools and that measurement is always a means to an end, never an end itself. In the final analysis, then, the value of any testing program depends upon the use of the results.

Every test that is administered to all students must be planned with a definite purpose in mind. The tests should be administered at grade levels that are appropriate to the kind of information yielded by the test in question. They should be administered at the time of the school year when their results can be most meaningful. Below is presented a testing program to be found in a typical high school. The inclusion of certain tests in this chart does not mean to suggest that these are the best tests available for the purposes listed. Each test, however, is a widely used instrument intended to elicit valuable data about individuals at the time that the test is scheduled. It is mandatory that the results of these testing programs be shared with teachers, preferably in a group meeting devoted to a discussion of the characteristics of students in a given school and how these students compare with other students of their age and grade level in the school district, the state, and the nation. Test data not shared with people to whom it can prove useful does not justify the time and expense involved in the development and maintenance of a comprehensive testing program. Other tests not listed on the chart might be administered to specific students (for example, an algebra aptitude test) as the needs of various students become evident.

2. *The Information Service.* The information service is primarily concerned with helping the student to learn more about the environment in which he will have to function as he matures into a responsible adult. There are basically three kinds of information a student must have: educational, vocational, and social.

Educational information is concerned with helping a student acquire information about the educational opportunities and educational requirements needed to realize certain levels of achievement in life. There are a number of ways of helping students to acquire such information. Students may receive this information from such literature as college catalogues, technical school bulletins, commercially available guides to educational opportunities, and a host of governmental publications. Educational information is also disseminated in group settings in group guidance classes, college day meetings, career days, and films produced by a number of sources. Perhaps the most effective method of helping students to acquire educational information is to have students who have participated in group activities discuss their educational plans individually with school counselors. Such discussions can take into account all the variables related to the students' level of development and probability of success in given educational endeavors. Three outstanding resources for acquiring detailed information about the dissemination of educational information are the books by Hoppock (1963); Norris, Zeran, and Hatch (1966); and Isaacson (1966).

Occupational information is concerned with assisting the student to gain knowledge about the world of work: what it is like now and what

## Testing Program of a Typical High School

| Grade | Test | Nature of Test | Major Purpose of Test | When Administered |
|---|---|---|---|---|
| 10th | Lorge-Thorndike Intelligence Test Verbal and Nonverbal | Scholastic aptitude | To measure ability in verbal and nonverbal areas of ability | Fall |
| 10th | Kuder Preference Record Form C | Measurement of interests in vocational areas | To assist in exploration of occupations | Fall |
| 11th | Iowa Tests of Educational Development | Achievement in nine areas | To assess achievement, identify deficiencies, evaluate for higher education | Winter |
| 11th | National Merit Scholarship Test | Achievement | Scholarship competition; compare with national norms | Spring |
| 11th and 12th | Preliminary Scholastic Aptitude | Aptitude | 11th-prediction of CEEB scores 12th-CEEB scores for college admission | Fall and Spring |
| 12th | General Aptitude Test Battery | Battery of tests for measuring aptitudes | Given by State Employment Service to non-college students | Spring |

it is probably going to be like in the foreseeable future. There are also many sources available to the student in this area. Perhaps the most reliable sources for the student and the counselor in learning about the world of work are the *Occupational Outlook Handbook* (1966) and a two-volume work edited by Hopke (1967). The sources listed under educational information also contain such material related to effective means of presenting occupational information to students.

Most secondary schools conduct career days in which representatives of some fifty or so careers of interest to members of the student body present talks to students about what is required to gain access to and advancement in a given career. It is essential that counselors inform students that they have an opportunity to discuss with the counselors any concerns or questions that arise as a result of knowledge or impressions acquired during the career day. In fact, it is common practice in many schools for the counselors to talk to *all* eleventh-graders about their post-high school plans. Counselors also frequently arrange field trips for individual students or for groups to visit work settings of interest to them.

Social information is also of importance to many students. Social information includes such things as boy-girl relations, personal habits, dress, appearance, etc. Many students do not learn these things at home. As is so often the case, the school must assume responsibility for getting those things done which other institutions have failed to do. Social information is sometimes presented as part of a career day when housewives talk to students about marriage and family life or when military representatives talk to male students about military obligations and alternatives to such obligations.

The information service has recently regained an important role in guidance programs. In a dynamic and rapidly changing world, it is crucial that the information considered by students as they attempt to make realistic plans for the future be as valid and as current as possible.

3. *The Counseling Service.* The counseling service is the heart of the guidance program. It is the service that is most directly related to effecting behavioral change and the service that places most demands upon the counselor. For the counseling service to be effective, it must have the following components: (1) there must be well-prepared personnel; (2) the time of the counselors must be devoted to the performance of those tasks for which counselors are specially prepared; and (3) there must be adequate facilities and resources for the counselor to do his work.

A guidance program is no better than the quality of the counselors who staff the program. Certification requirements for school counselors have increased substantially in the last ten years, and there is every reason to believe that they will increase further in the future. Ideally, all members of the professional staff involved in counseling activity should be certified. They should have engaged in practice counseling under supervision, had graduate work in all of the guidance services, and been deemed by counselor educators to have an adequate personality for counseling.

The problem of counselor selection has recently taken a quite different turn from the procedures recommended in the literature. Formerly, much of the selection in counseling was essentially self selection. A person, generally a classroom teacher decided that he wanted to become a counselor and went on to receive training. He then attempted to secure a counseling position. However, most selection now takes place as a result of the activity and identification procedures established by school administrators. Administrators, by and large, are now identifying their counseling needs several years ahead of time and sending teachers who they would like to see fill these positions on for graduate training in counselor education. In effect, administrators are now beginning to get in large numbers the kind of people they want as counselors. Whether this is good or bad must be determined by developments of the future. Certainly, this procedure insures that there will be relatively little conflict between counselors and administrators. The impact of this procedure on the ability and desire of the counselor to effect behavioral change may well be another matter.

Once the counseling service is staffed by adequately qualified counselors, the next task is to assign counselors in such a fashion that they may do their most effective work. This task is best handled by selecting one of the approaches to organization discussed earlier in this chapter.

Each counselor should have a private office in which to counsel with students. He should have appropriate guides to educational and occupational materials, and he should have filing space and materials to keep confidential records of his counseling activity. The notes that the counselor takes on his counseling interviews are not to be included in the cumulative record folder. These notes are kept in a locked file in the counselor's office. He should always consult his notes on previous interviews with a student before his next interview with him. This technique enables the counselor to demonstrate to the student that he remembers quite well what they have talked about in previous interviews, and it is external evidence of his interest in the student. A comprehensive treatment of the kinds of physical facilities that might be made available for the counselor can be found in Zeran and Riccio (1962).

At this point it is also appropriate to mention that the counselor should keep some record of the kind of problems presented by counselees. Such data will serve many purposes. For example, it will be useful in justifying the addition of new staff members or in informing the administration of the nature and scope of the counseling services actually being performed in the school. A counselee contact card which is easily completed, filed, and tabulated can be used to secure the data referred to above. This card is reproduced below. These cards can be completed by each counselor for each student he sees in a typical week or month of the school year, and projections can be made on the basis of these tabulations for what the counselors do for the entire school year.

## COUNSELEE CONTACT CARD

Student's Name:_____

<table>
<tr><td></td><td>Last</td><td>First</td><td>Middle</td></tr>
</table>

Counselor:_____

| Origin of First Interview: | *Interview No.* | *date* | *time* |
|---|---|---|---|
| (check proper category) | 1 | | |
| ( ) Referral | 2 | | |
| ( ) Voluntary | 3 | | |
| ( ) Called in | 4 | | |
| ( ) Other | 5 | | |
| If referral, please state source | 6 | | |
| and reason. | 7 | | |
| Source:_____ | 8 | | |
| Reason:_____ | 9 | | |

If voluntary, please state problem presented.
Problem:_____

### *NATURE OF PROBLEM*

*Educational:*
( ) Registration-schedule
( ) Schedule change
( ) Attendance — tardiness
( ) Scholastic failure
( ) Skill deficiency
( ) Over-achievement
( ) Under-achievement
( ) Course choice
( ) College choice

*Occupational:*
( ) Information
( ) Placement
( ) Choice
( ) *Testing:*
    ( ) Intelligence
    ( ) Achievement
    ( ) Personality
    ( ) Interest
( ) *Parent-Interview:*
    ( ) Home-visit
    ( ) School-visit
    ( ) Telephone
( ) *Teacher-Interview:*
    Teacher:_____

*Personal-Social:*
( ) Interests
( ) Emotional
( ) Motivational
( ) Discipline
( ) Social conflicts
( ) Home — family
( ) Financial
( ) Health

*Referral:*
( ) Reading clinic
( ) Speech clinic
( ) School nurse
( ) Psychological clinic
( ) Placement service
( ) Other

_____

4. *The Placement Service.* The placement service is essentially concerned with two kinds of placement. First, students are to be helped to move on to the next level of educational training. Second, students are desperately in need of assistance to make the big jump from the world of school to the world of work. Many schools routinely accept responsibility for placing their students in educational and vocational situations. There are, however, some educational personnel who look upon the placement function as mollycoddling. These people fail to realize that some students are simply incapable of making the transition from school to the work force without direct assistance from the school counselor. In fact, on a number of occasions it is actually necessary for the school counselor to set up appointments for students with employing officials and to transport the students to the interview setting. The school should assume a major role in the placement of students simply because it knows the student better than any other agency, with the possible exception of the home.

Intense involvement by the school counselor in the placement function does not simply aid the student; it is immensely valuable to the community in that it helps potential tax burdens to become taxpayers. In fact, some schools organize their placement services to meet the demands made on them by the industrial organizations within the community. It is not at all unusual for employers to view the school as a primary source for new employees.

Pupils need and deserve help in acting upon the decisions they make as a result of counseling. The school is in an excellent position to help students implement their decisions. Schools that meet this obligation are well regarded by the power structure in their communities, and as a result guidance programs receive much community support.

The responsibility for the placement of individuals in society is at this time a function that is not well defined. Local, state, federal, and private employment agencies have more experience, more money, and more information on occupational opportunities than do schools. But the school finds itself in a much better position than any of these agencies since it has so much data on and experience with the student. The procedures employed by the school to take advantage of its favorable position are of course, determined by the kind of community in which the school is located, the effectiveness of other placement agencies in the community, and numerous other factors. But if a school is to enjoy any success in developing an effective placement service, counseling personnel and teachers of relevant subjects must establish contacts in the community so that employers will notify school personnel of openings as soon as they occur.

*Community Resources*

Employers are but one group in the community who are of potential value to the school counselor as he attempts to implement his program of guidance services. In fact, one of the major weaknesses of most guidance programs is that for one reason or another most school counselors fail to avail themselves of the tremendous opportunities for community help available throughout the nation. Especially is this true in urban communities. Often the most effective step that a counselor can take in helping a given student resolve his difficulties is to refer him to a community agency equipped with special resources and personnel. This is true more often than not for students with whom the school has been ineffective. Below is a representative list of the kinds of community resources available in a community of more than 50,000 residents.

1. Adult and Child Guidance Clinics
2. Settlement Houses
3. Youth Opportunity Centers
4. Manpower Development and Training Centers
5. Council of Community Services
6. Religious Aid Societies
7. Goodwill Industries
8. Juvenile Court
9. Legal Aid Bureau
10. Department of Public Welfare
11. Urban League
12. Lions Club
13. Knights of Columbus
14. Public Health Service

This listing could of course be expanded considerably, but it suffices to demonstrate the plethora of resources available to the vast majority of school counselors in the nation.

*The Cost of Guidance Services*

The guidance services described heretofore and their implementation obviously cost a good deal of money. The total cost of a comprehensive guidance program is difficult to estimate. In estimating the cost of such a program, does one include the cost of heating and lighting the building? The cost of all materials, including classroom materials, that are relevant to guidance? The salaries of part-time counselors? These questions are difficult to answer, and there is little professional literature on the topic to serve as a guide. In some cases, the cost of guidance services is determined by adding the total square-feet of school space devoted to guidance activity and then multiplying this figure by the per-square-foot cost of constructing and maintaining the school plant. To this figure must be added the cost of special equipment employed in this space, the disposable materials involved, and the salaries and fringe benefits of personnel who man the guidance program. Perhaps the most comprehensive study of the cost of guidance services was conducted by the State Department of Guidance and Testing in Ohio (1964). The Ohio Study focused on schools in Ohio which in 1963 were participating in Title V-A of the National Defense Education Act of 1958. The most significant findings of the Ohio Study were the following:

1. The average per pupil cost for guidance services was $20.62.

2. This figure represented 5.34 percent of the total average school budget in the Ohio schools studied.

3. For every dollar spent on guidance materials in the guidance program, $19.23 was spent on guidance and clerical personnel required to operate the program.

Other studies dealing with the cost of guidance services and reported in the literature reveal that the cost of guidance services ranges from 1.4 percent to 8 percent of the total educational costs of the schools sampled in the various studies.

## Consultative Help

School counselors, especially beginning counselors, often are in need of professional consultation as they attempt to deal with the wide range of problems they confront in the schools. There are a number of sources to which they can turn for help. Perhaps the most common form of assistance received by counselors is service provided by most state departments of guidance and testing. These state agencies offer assistance with everything from initiating and developing guidance programs to participating in in-service training programs for school guidance workers. These services are generally provided free of charge or, at most, on a cost-reimbursement basis.

Another source for consultation is the counselor education staff at the nearest institution of higher education. Although this source of assistance is sometimes rendered free of charge, it is the usual practice for university consultants to receive from $50 to $100 a day for their services. Very often these fees can be met through participation in one or more of a number of federal programs. To make best use of consultative assistance, the school counselor should have in writing the precise nature of the concerns on which he wishes to receive assistance.

# 6

# Evaluation of
# Guidance Services

Growth implies change, and change, if it is to be planned, must be judged against some standard. This process of judging change against a standard is evaluation. Evaluation involves more than measurement and less than appreciation. As an inherently structured experience, education must also be judged. Hopefully, the school counselor will assume an active role in the evaluation of the guidance services. Performed wisely, it can serve as a core around which all guidance activities are planned and organized. Neglected or performed poorly, evaluation will be time consuming, frustrating and useless.

## Procedures for Evaluation

In fulfilling his professional function in evaluation, the school counselor should follow specific guidelines. He should develop an insight into the concept of evaluation itself and should be able to define the procedures for formal evaluation. This would include the elements of formal evaluation; means of surveying existing facilities, services, and attitudes; methods of evaluation; and implementation of results of evaluation. He should also be knowledgeable on the subject of change. He should be aware of the kinds of resources available to him as he attempts to organize and carry out an evaluation program. These resources will include information of the tools and techniques needed, materials and personnel available, and the means for developing skills in completing the process. He need not start with complete knowledge and skills but can plan to develop them as he proceeds through the experience.

### Informal Evaluation

Evaluation is an inherent part of any personal activity whether it be that of an individual, a total education program, or the guidance services of that program. It is a system of feedback through which individuals are able to position themselves in their environment and to acquire data about the effect of their behavior upon others and about the perceptions of others toward them. It is only through perceiving self-in-situation that an individual can predict the results of his present behavior and thus can guide his future action. For the most part this process is a natural one, often not conscious, and involves intellect as well as intuition, feelings, and emotions. It can at times be distorting. This process constitutes informal, subjective, personal evaluation.

Formal evaluation is an attempt to determine whether systemized behavior has produced desired outcomes. In practice, the evaluation of guidance services will be both formal and informal. Informally, the school counselor continuously evaluates the outcomes of his guidance services. In his counseling, for example, he uses a multitude of verbal and nonverbal cues to determine his progress with a student both during an interview and following. Even among the most effective counselors this evaluation process is seldom formalized. Effective evaluation does and should continue to take place through the counselor's own perceptual screen in informal ways.

However, this highly personalized form of evaluation should be constantly analyzed by the school counselor to insure that it is based in reality. He should develop skill in understanding himself and his idiosyncratic reactions to environmental press. He should be aware of his impact upon others and their perceptions of him as well as the distortions he gives his own experience. Since this personal evaluation will, in practice, constitute a part of the formal program of evaluation, the skills necessary to understanding one's self are usually a vital part of counselor training.

### Formal Evaluation

Formal evaluation procedures are a requisite part of any organized guidance program. These should be structured, made explicit, and should comprise an integral part of the development of the program itself. Formal evaluation may or may not involve research. Specific formal evaluation procedures will vary with each situation. However, as Zeran and Riccio (1962) state, three general elements of evaluation must be included in these procedures.

First, there must be a statement of the objectives of the service, program or activity to be evaluated. These objectives must be stated in such a fashion as to render them susceptible to observation and verification. Current thinking is that the objectives of the various school services should be stated in terms of behavioral outcomes that will be characteristic of, and noticeable in, the behavior of those who are to profit from the service. In guidance programs as well as in other programs, of course, the student is the principal agent to profit from the services, and, therefore, the objectives of the guidance services should be stated in terms of the desired behavioral outcomes of students.

Second, a list of activities or experiences should be structured as a means of enabling the student to develop the desired behavioral outcomes stated as objectives. A single activity, of course, could contribute to the attainment of more than one objective of the guidance program, whereas on the other hand, a number of activities might be required to help the student realize a single objective. This second phase of program development and evaluation must be well thought out by those planning the program. There must be a definite rationale for the inclusion of any activity or experience in the guidance program.

Third, procedures must be established to determine whether the activities and experiences structured in the second phase of the program development have actually resulted in the achievement of the expressed objectives of the program. This phase of program development is the heart of the evaluation process and is primarily concerned with deciding what kind of research methodology is necessary to learn the nature and the extent of the relationship between the first and the second phases of a comprehensive evaluation.

The school counselor should take an active part in the formulation of broad educational goals as well as the specific guidance responsibilities within them. The process of articulating objectives can be the most vital aspect of the total evaluation. This process should involve teachers, administrators, and guidance personnel at its core. To the extent that the institutional structure legitimately provides for student opinion, parent involvement, or lay participation, these should be included. Here the school counselor uses tacit intelligence regarding the power and influence structures, the social system, and the degree of potential contribution of others. Educational objectives, then, should encompass the guidance program objectives but should not necessarily be the same. The school counselor establishes for himself the program objectives that relate specifically to guidance activities. The description of these objectives can approximate the criteria to be used in evaluation.

## Outcomes and Objectives

### Student Outcomes

The criterion problem has long been a major difficulty confronting educational evaluators and guidance personnel. It has been called the greatest difficulty facing guidance, and to date no dramatic progress has been made in resolving it. Lists of evidences of objectives of guidance services are readily available in current literature. Shortcomings are widely discussed. Having thus apprised himself of potential lists of evidence and of the difficulty in selection, the school counselor must still make a personal decision based upon his own interpretation of the evidence as to what constitutes legitimate criteria.

Although more specific to counseling, Blocher (1965) reveals the difficulty in attempting to derive commonly accepted goals for guidance and counseling at both the operational and non-operational levels. Included here is a portion of the list of kinds of criteria he found in counseling evaluation studies.

Social Adjustment Criteria
    1. Adjustment rated by "experts"
    2. Reduction to disciplinary offenses
    3. Participation in group activities
Personality Criteria
    1. Congruence between self and ideal self-descriptions
    2. Changes on personality tests
    3. Ratings of personality change or adjustment
Vocational Criteria
    1. Specificity of vocational plans
    2. Job satisfaction
    3. Persistence in job
Educational Criteria
    1. Increase in grade-point average
    2. Correlation between grades and measured aptitude
    3. Entrance in college
Other Miscellaneous Criteria
    1. Client satisfaction
    2. Tendency to use public services
    3. Optimism about the future

At least a part of the current popularity of behavioral approaches to counseling must be attributed to its use of an intentionally well-defined link between counseling process and student outcome. In a field where much is taken on faith, concrete evidence that guidance practices do work is prized. However, since not all outcomes of effective guidance programs are currently measurable, to reduce all human development to such terms approaches bureaucracy.

A compromise position is one which would provide for three kinds of outcomes and/or behaviors as criteria for success. (1) Certain objectives can be translated directly into student behavior. Academic achievement, for example, is directly measurable by standardized tests and grades. (2) A second set of objectives can be indirectly ascertained through student behavior. Understanding of the world of work, for example, could be evaluated by the extent to which available occupational information is internalized by the student and evidenced by his verbal and non-verbal behavior. (3) A third set of objectives can only be assumed as a result of activities conducted. The efficacy of the assistance in the development of an identity through school experiences, for example, can only be assumed where the student is given numerous positive experiences with a significant adult. To the extent he is able, the school counselor should determine specific behavioral criteria for measuring student outcomes of the guidance program. Beyond that rigorous attempt, he should feel comfortable making legitimate assumptions about the effectiveness of some of his work.

### Other Outcomes

Not all outcomes of the guidance services involve student behaviors even though those objectives are primary. An effective guidance program can result in significant change in other ways. With regard to staff, greater teacher understanding of his students and familiarization with appraisal techniques might be noted. Effective guidance can result in a reorientation of staff from prevention to development where such an orientation does not already exist. Better student-teacher relationships and better parent-teacher cooperation can be anticipated from systematic guidance services. In general, it is hoped that a better emotional climate in the school will result from guidance procedures. At times the school counselor may find himself utilizing his counseling skills with teachers about their personal concerns.

The school counselor can direct some of his energies toward assisting parents in their relationships with their children. Although primary benefit is derived by the student, a concomitant outcome is a greater parental satisfaction. Assistance in locating and utilizing community resources can be provided parents; the use of these resources can improve the total family welfare. In specific instances, vocational as well as personal adjustment aid may be offered to parents. Unless this service has been planned as a part of the program, considerable caution should be used where the school counselor extends his service to parents outside the student relationship lest this drain his energies disproportionately.

Peters and Shertzer (1963) point out that a guidance program can affect the community as well as the school. Counselors can provide for an interpretation of the school to the citizenry through both private conferences and speaking engagements. They can participate in community projects and assist service organizations in school oriented activities. Cooperation with the local employment office and with industry in the vocational guidance program is obviously a great reward to the community as well as to the student. Follow-up studies can provide data for the community on the utilization of the manpower resources. The development of a positive attitude toward the community by the student and the realistic enhancement of opportunity locally is a valuable community outcome. On the other side of the ledger, the reduction of delinquency and crime can benefit the community economically as well as psychologically.

Thus guidance program evaluation should include an examination of other outcomes than those of student benefit. The same criterion problem exists as with student outcome. However, less rigid control need be exercised in evaluating these ancillary aspects of the program. The exception, of course, would be where specific research demands a more stringent and sophisticated approach.

### Survey of Services and Facilities

It is vital that a guidance program be based upon objectives that can be achieved within the framework of the current staff of the school and the opportunity that staff has in terms of time, curricular offering, facilities, budgetary matters, and personal resources to function at a level consonant with expressed objectives. Thus the application of a checklist for analyzing existing guidance services is advisable. This assessment should be accomplished through an appropriate guidance committee and should include an outside consultant. The instrument itself can be locally developed or may be extracted from readily available guidance sources. Schedule G of the *Evaluative Criteria* (1960) is a commonly used instrument for such purposes. Its limitation, as well as that of other checklists, is that it is merely an assessment tool.

Generally survey instruments require the evaluators to respond to a number of categories which comprise the guidance program. These responses are usually either "Yes" or "No" or points on a continuum which require the rater to determine the attitude, accessibility, extensiveness, or adequacy of the service or resource.

Perhaps the most profitable initial source for developing a survey instrument would be the ASCA proposed statements of policy and implementation. Suggestions for a program of guidance service would form a sound base for a locally useful survey tool. The general areas in this statement include the following. They would be useful in developing the facilities and resources section of the instrument.

| | |
|---|---|
| Personnel Administration | Out-of-Building Activities |
| Counseling Load and Assignment | In-Service Education |
| Supervision and Coordination | Research and Evaluation |
| Communication and Staff | Budget |
|    Participation | Space and Physical Facilities |
| Accessibility | Clerical and Secretarial |
| Ethical Standards |    Assistance |
| Confidentiality | Equipment and Materials |

The same proposed statement views potential school counselor functioning in the following ten areas and provides specificity in each. These could be used in the services section of the same instrument.

| | |
|---|---|
| Planning and Development of the | Referral Work |
|    Guidance Program | Placement |
| Counseling | Parent Help |
| Pupil Appraisal | Staff Counseling |
| Educational and Occupational | Local Research |
|    Planning | Public Relations |

The most effective survey instrument is viewed here as one that is locally developed but based upon the professional statement of school counselor role and one or more of the readily available excellent evaluative scales ( Hill, *et al.*, undated ).

## Survey of Attitudes and Awareness

### Staff

Attitudes of the staff toward the guidance services and the concepts inherent to the guidance process will determine the ultimate success of the guidance program. What the teacher perceives that the counselor does with the student vitally affects the teacher's perception of his own position relative to the student. It is not uncommon for teachers to view their own teaching competency in inverse ratio to the number of students they refer to the counselor and thus not use him. On the other hand, it is possible to develop an attitude wherein teachers take considerable pride in their ability to utilize available services to complement their own efforts.

Teacher attitude will also determine how the services will be used. There is little question today of the general acceptance of the developmental approach to guidance services. It is essential, therefore, that teachers understand the developmental contribution of the school counselor and use him in that way. Large numbers of studies conducted to ascertain teachers' perceptions of students' problems as reported on a problem checklist have revealed negative correlations between teachers' perceptions and student responses. Items most often checked by students were those in the category of Self-Centered Concerns. The category predicted by teachers as least common to student problems are generally Self-Centered Concerns. The school counselor can find this bit of datum highly useful in anticipating teachers' attitudes toward one of his most vital functions — dealing with self-centered concerns.

Just as a stock-taking of existing services and facilities should include an examination of the areas of the total guidance program, so should staff attitude be surveyed across the program. Both guidance staff and teachers should be in fairly close agreement as to the relative value of information service, placement, pupil appraisal, counseling, orientation and follow-up. Almost all recent studies indicate that counselors feel they should spend at least fifty percent of their time counseling. That teachers would question such an expenditure of energy is not hard to imagine. Viewed from the rules of social organization, the discrepant values assigned this role can cause disharmony, to say the least. Professionally, it is unsound not to be in agreement with those whose cooperation is essential for success.

Several attempts have been made on a state-wide basis to develop an instrument for surveying staff awareness of guidance services, e.g., Ohio, West Virginia, and Colorado. Local schools have also utilized staff survey attempts, although staff surveys are not as common as student polls. To date it would appear that the school counselor's use of Q-sorts, problem checklists, unpublished instruments, and locally developed techniques provides the most promise for surveying teacher attitudes. In attempting such a task, the school counselor would be advised to take the following precautions. (1) He should involve a teacher committee in the operation from its very inception. (2) He should restrict his survey to those areas or services about which he can realistically bring about change if a need for change is indicated through the survey. (3) He should not limit himself to questionnaire means alone. (4) He should be clearly aware of the inherent dangers of providing a platform for the venting of hostility or negative feeling that may exist on the part of some teachers. On the other hand, he should also recognize the value of a properly conducted open forum on attitudes and opinions.

### Students

Student attitude surveys are more common than staff surveys. These include surveys of current students as well as follow-up studies of graduates. A program for the evaluation of guidance in Ohio was developed by the State Department of Education (1962). Out of this study evolved an instrument for surveying student guidance awareness, "Student Inventory of Guidance Awareness," and a number of similar extensions of the study in local schools. Almost all the Ohio state universities involve some counselor trainees in studies of this nature.

An often neglected useful function of the student evaluation is to examine variables which describe the student body. Rather than simply stopping at the answer to the question "What do students think of the guidance program?" answers should be sought to "Who thinks what about the guidance program?" The usual ways of categorizing by grade, sex, marks and curricula do not suffice as a complete answer. Other categories can be investigated and these used to analyze both the student body and the guidance program. As a part of basic categorization it would appear essential to find out the number of previous contacts the student has had with a counselor; the nature of these contacts, whether group, individual, class, or informal; whether it was for counseling, information giving, or other purposes; whether he was self-referred, teacher referred, or routinely contacted. It would also be necessary to know the nature of his utilization of other guidance services. In one survey a school counselor found that when students were asked to rank educational occupations among others along a prestige dimension, those students who had a positive contact with the counselor ranked the job title of counselor just below that of principal. Those students who had a negative contact with the counselor ranked him not only below the teacher but below the electrician as well.

## Methods of Evaluation

Methods used in evaluating the outcomes of guidance are limited only by the imagination possessed by the school counselor. Generally, these can be classified under several headings: follow-up, observation techniques, survey methods, controlled experimentation, and case study.

### Follow-up

The most common form of evaluation to be found in high school guidance programs is the follow-up study. The follow-up study is conducted by postcard or questionnaire and yields a wealth of data which is of service in learning what has happened to students who have been the products of the school in general and the guidance program in particular. Follow-up techniques are described in detail in Norris, Zeran, and Hatch (1966). Below is a list of problems which illustrate the kinds of tasks to which follow-up techniques lend themselves:

1. To evaluate curriculum needs of students and the need for changes in course content.
2. To discover whether certain phases of vocational education are needed.
3. To determine reasons why students leave school before graduation and characteristics of potential drop-outs.
4. To gather occupational and other information.
5. To determine the degree of realism of occupational choices made in high school.
6. To identify reasons why capable students fail to enter college or additional post-high school training.
7. To gather post-high school educational and other training information.
8. To identify facilities used by former students to obtain employment.
9. To identify the need for area community colleges.
10. To identify counseling tasks.
11. To evaluate counseling services.
12. To evaluate other guidance services and needs for future planning.
13. To evaluate the predictive value of guidance tools.

## Observation

Evaluation by observation can be conducted by the counselor, a staff member, or an outside consultant. This can be an informal process left to the discretion of the observer or may be conducted according to a pre-planned schedule. Significant samples of on-going behavior are recorded and interpreted by the observer. These will usually include observations of the individuals involved in the guidance services as they perform their duties, individual and group discussions with staff and students, and an examination of the extent and effects of the guidance services. Generally the observations are conducted with a specific purpose in mind for each instance, but at times "open" observations are made with the intent of drawing some impressions following the experience. Follow-up interviews can be held and conferences conducted later for the collection of further data and impressions or the reinterpretation of the original ones.

While obviously subjective in nature, it must be remembered that subjectivity is legitimate. Caution should be taken, however, to use information gathered through observation with somewhat less enthusiasm than with that obtained through more controlled methods. Perhaps one of the most convincing arguments for including observation in the evaluation process is that it is likely to occur anyway.

Deliberate inclusion in the program of evaluation provides a greater certainty that information obtained will be more easily identified and possibly more valid if it is more controlled. Its proper place in the total evaluation program thus can be insured.

### Questionnaire and/or Survey

Because of their apparent and deceiving ease, questionnaires have suffered considerable misuse as a survey technique. A carefully developed questionnaire can provide generally useful information; a poorly constructed one is worse than no instrument at all. Through the ordinary use of the questionnaire, it is virtually impossible to ascertain anything except that which the respondent wishes to reveal. At best the administrator of the instrument can only feel comfortable about the degree of willingness of the respondent to express opinions or give facts of which his data ultimately consist. The proposition that "What Johnny says about Mary often tells more about Johnny than about Mary" is true not only for the observation but for the questionnaire approach to evaluation as well.

Too often not enough data are gathered about respondents to be able to evaluate their responses according to their own biases. Usually such information about respondents includes only the more obvious objective facts and not the more difficult to determine attitudinal or experiential ones. Follow-up procedures can insure some degree of validity of results while adding more information for the general interpretation of elicited information. Caution should always be taken when using the questionnaire to collect and report opinions and attitudes about guidance services or information on the performance of guidance duties as perceptions rather than facts. These should be so labeled. Despite the cautions stressed in the use of this type of instrument, its popularity will not soon diminish. With the increased availability of data processing equipment, more extensive studies can be anticipated. Many of these will continue to make major contributions to guidance.

### Controlled Experimentation

All controlled experimentation can be considered research, but not all research need be controlled experimentation. Several texts state a case for conducting research which is not limited to experimentation and accurately point to the utility of these studies in improving guidance services. There is considerable room for the school counselor to conduct valid research without requiring a prohibitive level of statistical or research sophistication.

The most serious problems encountered in guidance and counseling research seem to be the criterion problem and the control problem. The criterion, or the dependent variable, used for measuring success in studies of complex human behavior in non-laboratory settings presents universal concern. This problem has received consideration elsewhere in this section. The control problem is represented by the difficulties encountered in defining the relationship between cause and effect. Many of the independent variables in guidance and counseling research cannot be isolated and controlled. Such research usually involves change or growth. The differences noted not only may be affected by an intervening variable, but may well be the result of natural maturation.

The sampling problem in conducting research as evaluation rests primarily in the difficulties encountered in identifying adequate research groups and in matching them. Further, the conclusions drawn from such studies can usually only apply to the institution or segment of the institution from which the sample was drawn. Generalizations for evaluative purposes are thus highly tenuous.

Nevertheless, controlled experimentation as a part of the evaluation program is highly valuable. Suggested designs are offered in a number of texts to give the counselor some direction in his own program (Hatch and Stefflre, 1958). The school counselor can serve as both a producer of research and a consumer of research. He both contributes to and keeps apprised of the current findings of others faced with similar if not identical problems and concerns. He learns to critically examine the findings as reported in the current journals devoted to reporting research findings. He can wisely spend time in in-service training using research, including controlled experimentation, as a vehicle. He can use research as an on-going program of investigation and improvement.

### Case Study

The case study technique as a non-experimental method can be applied to individuals, school programs, school systems, and communities. The case study technique generally proceeds by accumulating extensive relevant information on a specific student or problem. It is comprised of a collection of all available evidence — social, psychological, health, biographical, environmental, and vocational — that promises to explain a single instance, whether individual, program, school, or community. This accumulation of data provides for careful analysis of all the resources, instruments, and processes which can be brought to bear upon that specific instance.

The approach is expansive in that in the process of accumulating data, the participants look outward toward the existing services and their relationships. They gain insight into these services in terms of their comprehensiveness and interrelatedness. It is intensive in that an application must be made to a specific instance and its efficacy judged. Thus, through posing a specific question on a specific student and bringing to bear all the available resources, the case study makes it possible to analyze the general setting of the school, its policies and practices, all available information, the roles and responsibilities of the staff, supportive agencies, and any other information desired by a participant.

# BIBLIOGRAPHY

American Personnel and Guidance Association, "The counselor: professional preparation and role." *Personnel and Guidance Journal*, Vol. 42, 1964, 536–541.

American School Counselor Association, *Proposed Statement of Policy for Secondary School Counselors and Proposed Guidelines for Implementation of the ASCA Statement of Policy for Secondary School Counselors.* Washington, D.C.: American Personnel and Guidance Association, 1964.

Association for Counselor Education and Supervision, *Counselor education: a progress report on standards.* Washington, D.C.: APGA, 1962.

Blocher, Donald, *Developmental Counseling.* New York: Ronald, 1965.

Brizendine, Rayalene, "An analysis of literature concerning the school dropout." Unpublished master's thesis, Ohio State University, 1963.

Byrne, Richard, *The School Counselor.* Boston: Houghton-Mifflin, 1963.

Coleman, James, *The Adolescent Society.* New York: Free Press, 1961.

Dillon, Harold J., *Early school leavers: a major educational problem.* New York: National Child Labor Committee, 1949.

Douvan, Elizabeth, and Adelson, Joseph, *The Adolescent Experience.* New York: Wiley, 1966.

Erikson, Erik H., *Childhood and Society.* New York: W. W. Norton, 1950.

*Evaluative criteria: schedule g. guidance services.* Washington, D.C.: Cooperative Study of Secondary School Standards, 1960.

Friedenberg, Edgar Z., *The Vanishing Adolescent.* Boston: Beacon Press, 1959.

Fullmer, Daniel W., and Bernard, Harold W., *Counseling: Content and Process.* Chicago: Science Research Associates, 1964.

Getzels, J. W., and Jackson, Phillip, *Creativity and Intelligence.* New York: Wiley, 1962.

Goffman, Irving, *Encounters: two studies in the sociology of interaction.* Indianapolis: Bobbs-Merrill, 1961.

Goode, W. J., "A theory of role strain." *American Sociological Review*, Vol. 25, 1960, pp. 483–496.

Goslin, Paul A., *The School in Contemporary Society.* Chicago: Scott Foresman, 1965.

Havighurst, Robert J., *Human Development and Education*. New York: Longmans-Green, 1953.

Hill, George E., *Management and Improvement of Guidance*. New York: Appleton-Century-Crofts, 1965.

————, *et al.*, *The Guidance Resources Inventory*. Athens, Ohio: The Center for Educational Service, Ohio University, undated.

Hopke, William E., ed., *Encyclopedia of Careers and Vocational Guidance*, 2 vols. Garden City, New York: Doubleday, 1967.

Hoppock, Robert, *Occupational Information*. New York: McGraw-Hill, 1963.

Horrocks, John E., *The Psychology of Adolescence*. Boston: Houghton Mifflin, 1962.

Irelan, Lola M., *Low Income Life Styles*. Washington, D.C.: U.S. Department of Health, Education, and Welfare, 1966.

Isaacson, Lee E., *Career Information in Counseling and Teaching*. Boston: Allyn and Bacon, 1966.

Kough, Jack, and DeHaan, Robert F., *Helping Students with Special Needs*. Chicago: Science Research Associates, 1956.

MacKinnon, Donald W., "What makes a person creative." *Theory Into Practice*, Vol. 55, 1966 pp. 152–156.

"Magnitude of the American educational establishment, 1966–67." *Saturday Review of Literature*, October 15, 1966.

Maslow, Abraham, *Motivation and Personality*. New York: Harper and Row, 1954.

Mathewson, Robert H., *Guidance Policy and Practice*. New York: Harper and Row, 1962.

Matika, Francis N., and Sheerer, Rebecca, "Are the causes of dropouts ex-. cuses?" *Bulletin of the National Association of Secondary School Principals*, Vol. 44, 1962, pp. 40–44.

Nordstrom, Carl, Friedenberg, Edgar Z., and Gold, Hilary, *Society's Children*. New York: Random House, 1967.

Norris, Willa, Zeran, Franklin, and Hatch, Raymond, *The Information Service in Guidance*. Chicago: Rand McNally, 1966.

*Occupational Outlook Handbook*, Bulletin 1450. Washington, D.C.: U.S. Department of Labor, 1966–67.

Parsons, Talcott, "Youth in the context of American society." *Daedalus*, Vol. 91, 1962, pp. 97–123.

Peters, Herman J., and Shertzer, Bruce, *Guidance: program development and management*. Columbus, Ohio: Charles E. Merrill, 1963.

*Program for evaluation of guidance*. Columbus, Ohio: State Department of Guidance and Testing, 1962.

Riccio, Anthony C., and Weathersby, Keith, "The educational backgrounds of certificated school counselors in Ohio." *Guidance*, Vol. 3, 1964, pp. 1–7.

Riessman, Frank, *Helping the Disadvantaged Pupil to Learn More Easily.* Englewood Cliffs, N.J.: Prentice-Hall, 1966.

Roeber, Edward C., *The school counselor.* Washington, D.C.: Center for Applied Research in Education, 1963.

Sarbin, Theodore R., "Role theory." In Gardner Lindsey, ed., *Handbook of Social Psychology,* Vol. 1. Cambridge, Mass.: Addison-Wesley, 1954, pp. 223–258.

Secord, Paul W., and Backman, Carl W., *Social Psychology.* New York: McGraw-Hill, 1964.

State Department of Guidance and Testing, *Cost of guidance services.* Columbus, Ohio: State Department of Guidance and Testing, 1964, mimeographed.

Super, Donald, "The professional status and affiliations of vocational counselors." In Henry Borow, ed., *Man in a World of Work.* Boston: Houghton Mifflin, 1964.

Torrance, E. Paul, *Constructive Behavior: Stress, Personality and Mental Health.* Belmont, Cal.: Wadsworth, 1965.

———, "Nurture of creative talents." *Theory Into Practice,* Vol. 5, 1966, pp. 170–173.

Tyler, Leona, *The Work of the Counselor.* New York: Appleton-Century-Crofts, 1961.

Washburne, Chandler, "Conflicts between educational theory and structure." In Frederick Cyphert, Earl Harmer, and Anthony C. Riccio, eds., *Teaching in the American Secondary School.* New York: McGraw-Hill, 1964.

Wrenn, C. Gilbert, *The Counselor in a Changing World.* Washington, D.C.: American Personnel and Guidance Association, 1962.

Zeran, Franklin, and Riccio, Anthony C., *Organization and Administration of Guidance Services.* Chicago: Rand McNally, 1962.

# INDEX

## DATE DUE

| SE 18 '99 | | |
|---|---|---|
| NO 07 06 | | |
| | | |
| | | |
| | | |
| | | |
| | | |
| | | |
| | | |
| | | |
| | | |
| | | |
| | | |
| | | |
| GAYLORD | | PRINTED IN U.S.A. |